How to Get
BETTER
GRADES
And
Have More Fun!

How to Get BETTER GRADES

And Have More Fun!

STEVE DOUGLASS
WITH AL JANSSEN

HOW TO GET BETTER GRADES
AND HAVE MORE FUN
by Steve Douglass
with Al Janssen

Published by:

Success Factors
c/o Integrated Resources
100 Sunport Lane
Orlando, FL 32809
1-800-729-4351
Prod# 1201e

Second printing, January 1986
Third printing, February 1987
Fourth printing, August 1989
Fifth printing, July 1992
Sixth printing, September 1994
Seventh printing, October 1995

Library of Congress Cataloging-in-Publication Data

Douglass, Stephen B.

How to Get Better Grades And Have More Fun.

1. Study, Method of.
2. College student orientation.
   I. Janssen, Al.
   II. Title.
   LB2395.D66   1985   378'.1702812   85-16451
   ISBN 0-89840-090-2 (pbk.)

FOR MORE INFORMATION, WRITE:

L.I.F.E. — P.O. Box A399, Sydney South 2000, Australia
Campus Crusade for Christ of Canada — Box 300, Vancouver, B.C., V6C 2X3, Canada
Campus Crusade for Christ — Pearl Assurance, 4 Temple Row, Birmingham, B2 5HG, England
Lay Institute for Evangelism — P.O. Box 8786, Auckland 3, New Zealand
Campus Crusade for Christ — P.O. Box 240, Colombo Court Post Office, Singapore 9117
Great Commission Movement of Nigeria — P.O. Box 500, Jos, Plateau State Nigeria, West Africa
Campus Crusade for Christ International — 100 Sunport Lane, Orlando, FL 32809, U.S.A.

to Debbie
and
to Joshua

CONTENTS

ACKNOWLEDGMENTS

To Judy and JoAnn, our wives, for their loving patience and encouragement.

To Tim Jaycox and Larry Thompson for their graphic contributions to communication.

To Cathy Pletzke, Shirley Scott, Denise Svendsen and Diana Winsor for their excellent typing and general assistance.

To Phyllis Alsdurf, Sara Anderson and Jean Bryant for their able editing.

To Bobb Biehl for his creativity with the book title.

A WORD FROM THE AUTHORS

Would you like to do better in school? Do you think that the only way is to take a lot more time and rob you of all your fun?

If so, then this book is for you. You *can* get better grades than you are now getting. In this book you will discover how. Selected, proven techniques will help you learn, not just go for grades. It probably won't take any more of your time. It may take much less.

How can this be? You'll hear it from Dave. He is a graduate student who has learned from experience. See if you can identify with Al and Joanne. They are undergraduate students who want to improve. Learn as they learn — week by week as they face real-life student problems.

And don't worry about putting it all together. We do that for you at the end of the book — all in one chart. Enjoy yourself as you read. It'a a story about people like you.

Now. . . you are about ready to get better grades and have more fun.

1

THE OFFER: GET BETTER GRADES AND HAVE MORE FUN

At least a dozen college sophomores were sitting around the student union lounge on a drizzly afternoon. It was the first week of the fall term and they were comparing prospects for the new school year.

When Joanne mentioned that she had Professor Bolger for economics, there was a collective groan. Tom was most sympathetic, though: "He's the toughest *C* on campus."

"I don't think that old bear's ever given an *A*," said Kent.

"And how would you know?" Perry asked. "You've never even sniffed an *A*." Everyone laughed, for Kent was known as one of the school's most dedicated partyers.

"If you want an *A* in Bolger's class," Kent insisted, "you'll have to study 25 hours a day. Even then, there's no guarantee."

"Hey, Sally" Perry spoke to one of the girls. "What are you taking this term?"

"Literature, French, and psychology. I'm pulling for a *B* average again, as long as it doesn't interfere with my social life."

"Nothing interferes with that," laughed Kent. "You only go around once in life. Why spoil it by having to study when you can have a good time?"

"And you'll be lucky to be in school next term," Tom quipped.

"Yeah, but what a way to go!" Kent retorted. "So how does your semester look?"

"It doesn't seem to matter what I take, or how hard I study, I can't seem to get better than a *C* plus," he answered.

"See what I mean?" said Kent. "You might as well loosen up a little."

"Now wait a minute!" It was Glenn. A pre-med major, he usually was quiet so everyone turned to hear what he had to say. "You get out of school what you put into it. No pain, no gain. That's what I say."

"Did you pull a 4.0 last year?" asked Sally.

Glenn blushed at the question. He wanted to be part of the group, but that was hard because he spent so many hours studying. "Glenn, old buddy," said Al, a basketball player, "I'll bet you didn't do one fun thing all last year."

"I went to a concert," he protested.

"Well, ex-cuse me," Al said with exaggeration. "So you study twenty hours a day. But there's more on this campus than books. You need to live a little. Find a girl friend. That will give balance to those studies!"

"That's all well and good," Joanne chimed in, "but I sympathize with Glenn. I have a job, and between work and studies, there isn't much time for fun."

"You got to *make* the time, Joanne," said Tim, who was on academic probation.

"I've got my boy friend."

"Yeah, and all you two do is study."

Lee, who was active in campus government, defended Joanne. "Tim, if you'd spend less time playing cards and a little more time in the books, you wouldn't be in danger of flunking out of school."

"Yeah," added Perry, "you've already cut three classes, and it's only the first week!"

Tim shrugged his shoulders. "Hey, I'm just getting warmed up."

"I don't know about you guys, but I know what I want in life." John, a fraternity man, was majoring in business administration. "What are we here for anyway? We're preparing for a career. There's got to be a balance. You can't leave here only with academic knowledge. You need people skills, too."

"You seem a little stronger in the people skills," laughed Al.

"And you don't exactly have the toughest major, John" added Glenn.

"Well, you can't have everything. I'm happy if I get a *B* average and keep my scholarship. You need time to do other things."

"My parents aren't satisfied with less than straight *A*'s," said Sue. "Since they're paying my way, that eliminates a lot of extra curricular activities for me."

"Excuse me!" No one had noticed just when the tall man, who appeared to be in his thirties, had joined the outskirts of the group. "I couldn't help overhearing your conversation. Could I ask you something?"

There was a moment of surprised silence. It was Lee who suggested that the man proceed.

"If I hear what you're saying, some of you feel that in order to learn, to get good grades, and to succeed in school, you can't have a lot of fun. Others are saying that you're not willing to give up the fun, so you have to sacrifice the grades. Is that right?"

"I guess so," said Lee. Several others nodded their heads in agreement.

"Well, I've found in my experience that you can have both. You *can* get good grades and still have fun."

"And what are you doing here in school?" asked Tom. "Shouldn't a man of your age have graduated by now?"

The man laughed, not at all offended. "I graduated ten years ago and I've been in business since then. I've come back here now to finish my MBA degree."

"So, Mister. . .?" Sally paused.

"Dave," the man answered.

"So, Dave, you must be a genius," she continued.

"I'm no genius," Dave offered, "but I have learned a few basic skills. I was able to place in the top ten percent of my graduating class, yet I played basketball, was involved in student government and participated in many campus activities. Besides, I learned the right things from my college experience which I've been able to apply in business. So I didn't just get better grades; I really learned."

"I've got it! You never sleep," said Kent. "That's an unfair advantage."

"I average seven hours a night. But let me ask you," Dave looked at Kent, "how many hours do you study on an average day?"

"I don't know. Probably three or four."

"Be serious," Perry joked.

"And how were your grades last year?" Dave asked.

"I managed a *C* average."

Dave turned to Sally. "You said you had a *B* average last year. How many hours do you study a day?"

"About the same. Three or four."

"Tim, what about you?"

"I try to study three hours a day."

Several in the group laughed. "It's not doing you much good!" said Al.

Dave smiled but quickly made his point. "It seems all three of you study about the same number of hours each day. Yet Sally got a *B* average, Kent a *C*, and Tim's on probation. So apparently the time you spend studying doesn't make the difference.

"What about intelligence?" He pointed to several students, asking them to compare their intelligence level and grade point average. Some said their intelligence was average, others were willing to admit they were above average. Dave noted that two students with above-average intelligence had *C* averages the previous year. Two others had *B*'s. Glenn had straight *A*'s. "It appears that intelligence isn't the only, perhaps not even the primary, factor in getting good grades."

"Okay, so what's the difference?" asked Lee. "How come you can do so much better?"

"I've learned that a few basic principles and techniques, faithfully practiced, will yield most of the benefit. When they apply these principles, most people will get good grades *and* have more fun."

Joanne saw her opportunity. "Do you think I could get an *A* out of Bolger?"

"Well, he might be a real challenge," Dave answered with a chuckle. "However, I would be willing to make this guarantee: If you faithfully apply the principles I'm talking about, your grades will improve by a half to a full point, probably without requiring any more of your time. Of course, Glenn, you can't improve on straight *A*'s. But these principles might help you find time for a little more fun."

"Where can I read up on this?" asked Al. "I haven't seen anything about it in the bookstore."

"I don't know of such a book," Dave admitted. "But if you're interested, I'd be willing to spend a little time with you and show you what I've learned."

"I've got to read twenty-five books for my literature class," Joanne interjected. "How can I read them all and have time left for anything else?"

"Good question. That's a lot of reading. How many hours a day do you read?"

"I don't know. At least three. Sometimes a lot more."

"If you read three hours a day, would you be interested in learning how to cover the same amount of material in half the time with equal or better comprehension?"

"Sure! Who wouldn't?" she laughed. But she didn't believe that was possible.

"I've got to write a paper a week," said Tom. "I'll pay you to write them!"

"Way to think, Tom!" laughed Al.

"I've got a better idea," Dave said. "Do you know *how* to approach writing your papers?"

Lee answered for Tom. "Yeah, he waits till the night before, then panics!"

"Maybe if you developed a definite plan for writing those papers, you could remove a lot of the anxiety about them. That would let you be more creative, and you'd naturally have better papers."

"Hey, it's class time!" said Perry. Several other students looked at their watches and began to leave. All of them seemed to enjoy the discussion. After all, it was nice to dream about getting better grades and having time for more fun too. But they didn't really believe it could be done. Even if this man could help them, how could they afford to spend any time with him when they were already so busy? No, the majority would continue in their current study practices, developed through years of habit, and hope for the best.

But Al and Joanne didn't leave with the crowd. They were curious about Dave's offer to help — and the guarantee he made.

"Look, I'm interested in what you had to say," said Al. "I mean, about doing a few basics to free up time. Could we talk some more?"

"I'd like to know more about those skills," said Joanne. "Especially the reading."

"I'd love to meet with you," said Dave with a smile. "How about tomorrow afternoon?"

"It'll have to be at two o'clock," said Al. "I'm playing basketball at three."

"That's a good time for me," said Joanne.

"Then it's settled," said Dave. "I'll meet you in the coffee shop."

Dave watched them leave. *This will be fun,* he thought as he turned and headed for his apartment. *They seem eager to learn. It looks like they have what it takes to become 80/20 Students.*

2

THE SECRET:
THE 80/20 RULE

Joanne, Al and Dave went through the cafeteria line and bought soft drinks. Al joked about also buying two donuts. "I'm always hungry when I'm playing basketball," he said as they sat at a round table near the corner of the cafeteria. "And I'm always playing basketball."

"Why don't you tell me a little bit about yourself," asked Dave.

"Well, I'm handsome, athletic, and humble!" he said, and Dave and Joanne joined in the laughter. "I'm a sophomore, majoring in engineering. I was a walk-on in basketball last year, and this year the coach says I have a good chance to make the varsity."

"What about you, Joanne?"

"I'm a sophomore, too, a liberal arts major. There's not a whole lot to tell you. I work part-time at Burger Boy, and I spend a little time with Jim, my boy friend. And I love to read, though 25 books in a term is a bit much even for me. Maybe if I didn't have any other classes. . .but I've got Dr. Bolger for economics. I guess you've heard of him."

"Sounds like he's a tough one. How did he earn his reputation?"

"It's like he has no understanding that we are taking other classes. There is nothing for him besides economics. You could spend three to five hours a day easily on his homework assignments alone. And as you heard, he almost never gives an *A*."

"I haven't told you much about myself," Dave said. "That

might be helpful before we launch in. I'm married and have two children. My wife's name is Mary and my sons are John and Joshua. We live about a mile from campus in an apartment we've rented for the year. As I said yesterday, I'm in the final year of the MBA program. I graduated from State Tech. . ."

"State Tech!" interrupted Al. "I'm impressed. What was your major?"

"Engineering, just like you. I managed to graduate with a 3.5 grade point average. And you already know, I played basketball and belonged to a fraternity. Since graduation, I've been working for a large electronics firm. Three years ago, they made me the vice president."

"Doesn't sound like you need any more schooling," said Al.

"Actually, I've never stopped learning. My philosophy is to continue to study, even when I'm not in school. I take management seminars and read a wide variety of books. Ten years ago, I could have done the studies for my master's, but the work experience has shown me what I really need to know. Over the years, I took several courses toward the degree; then the company encouraged me to take a year and concentrate on it full time. So I'm on what you might call a study sabbatical. Now let me ask each of you a question. What would you like to get out of our time together?"

Joanne spoke first. "I mentioned the reading yesterday. Actually, what really bothers me is that in high school I was a straight A student. I graduated fourth in my class. Last year, I managed only one A, the rest B's except for one C — first time I ever remember getting a C. I've never studied so hard in my life, yet it doesn't seem to be enough. Plus, I work four afternoons a week, so there's little chance to relax."

"So you'd like to learn how to improve your study skills in order to maintain an A average, and maybe have a little more time for some fun?"

Joanne nodded her head in agreement.

"What about you, Al? What would you like to get out

of this time?"

"I'd like to improve my grades, too. I don't need all *A*'s, but I had only a *C* average last year. I'd like to bring it up to a *B*, yet I don't want to sacrifice basketball. If I'm going to make the team, I have to practice two to three hours a day. I'm also involved in a fraternity, and that takes time."

"I've just given you your first lesson. What I did is something I do at the start of every meeting, whether it's in business or school. The first thing I do is determine the objective of the meeting."

Dave reached into his thin briefcase and pulled out several three-by-five cards. "I believe I can help you achieve your objectives. However, you didn't develop your present study habits overnight, so it'll take some time to develop new habits. If you're interested, I'd be willing to meet with you once a week during this term. That way we can cover two or three principles at a time, and it will give you a chance to try them out. Each week we can review your progress, and I can answer questions and help you with any problems you're having."

"So you'll act kind of like a mentor?" asked Al.

"That's not a bad way to put it."

"Before you start, I've got a question," noted Joanne. "You said there are only a few things that make the difference in getting good grades and also having more fun. I couldn't get that out of my mind last night. Is that really true?"

"Your question gives us an excellent place to start," said Dave handing Al and Joanne several index cards. "I'd like you to write each principle I give you on a separate card. That will help you remember what we discuss.

"Now, Joanne, to answer your question, I believe there are a limited number of important skills necessary for success in school. I call it the 80/20 Rule. When I was an undergraduate student I evaluated the results from my school activities. I discovered that about 80 percent of my results came from about 20 percent of my activity. The other 80 percent of my activity contributed only about 20 percent to my results in learning and grades.

"That is not a new observation. Have you ever heard of the Pareto Principle?"

Al and Joanne responded with blank looks.

"Vilfredo Pareto was an Italian economist and sociologist in the nineteenth century. He observed that the significant items in a group of items are normally just a small portion of the total items in the group.

"Joseph Juran, a management expert, coined the terms 'vital few' and 'trivial many.' He and others applied the Pareto Principle to management situations in business. For example, they found that normally 80 percent of the sales resulted from about 20 percent of the product line.

"I have just applied this same principle to my studies and called it the 80/20 Rule."

THE 80/20 RULE—
80 PERCENT OF THE BENEFIT FROM SCHOOL CAN BE DERIVED FROM DOING THE RIGHT 20 PERCENT OF THE ACTIVITY WELL

Al and Joanne wrote the sentence down on their cards. When they were finished, Dave amplified. "Of course, the trick is to learn the right 20 percent. Now that doesn't mean you'll do 80 percent less work. What I'm suggesting is that you concentrate more on the 20 percent of the activity that will yield the greatest benefit. The idea is to cut out some of the non-productive activity in the learning process and focus on that which is productive. Do that and you will learn more and get better grades."

"I don't understand," said Al. "Are you saying that not everything we do in school is of equal benefit?"

"That's right, Al. Different activities vary widely in how they contribute to success in school. For example, how productive do you think it is to read your textbook when you are extremely sleepy?"

"Well, it is very productive for putting me to sleep," laughed Al, "but not for learning."

"Exactly. Yet many people study most often at their non-alert times. Then they wonder why it takes so much time to get done and why they don't remember much. Not all study times are equal in value.

"What's more, not all participation in class is equal either. Let me illustrate. In my graduate program, all of our courses are taught by the case-study method rather than by lecture. Basically, we learn by solving problems. Our homework is to study a particular business problem. The case is presented in ten to twenty pages. Then we discuss it in class, with the instructor guiding the discussion.

"Generally there are four stages of discussion. First is the leadoff stage. Someone is called on, or volunteers, to make an initial presentation of the case. To do this well, you need to be highly prepared, and the reward is medium to high. By reward, I mean the benefit you gain in terms of learning as well as your grade.

"The second stage is the 'cheap shot' stage. It's a direct response to what you've just heard in class. You can react to any idea and point out the flaws in the leadoff argument. The preparation is low, but the reward is also low; the professor knows you just have to listen in class.

"Third is the construction stage. Now the prof is looking for answers. If you've done some preparation, you can throw a plank into some portion of the solution platform. Medium work, medium reward.

"The last stage is summary. It usually occurs in the last five minutes of class, when we show what lessons we have learned from solving the problem. Here is the highest reward.

Do you know why?"

Al shrugged his shoulders.

"Is it because it demonstrates your understanding?" Joanne tentatively asked.

"Exactly! It demonstrates comprehension and learning. That's what the teacher wants to see. And how much work is it? Naturally, we need to do some reasonable study of the case before class — but not nearly as much as if we're leading off — and then we need to pay attention to the discussion. Now if I'm applying the 80/20 principle, on which of the four stages should I concentrate?"

"The last one," said Al. "It has the highest ratio of benefit to cost."

"That's exactly right, Al! Do you see what I'm illustrating? It's interesting that many students in the MBA program study two or three times the number of hours I do. One guy always likes to lead off. There are a couple of students who are eager to demonstrate their solution to some aspect of the case. Obviously I'm involved in the other stages, but I participate in summary as often as possible. Why? Because it provides the highest reward per hour of my effort. The professor sees I've comprehended the lesson, which helps my grade, plus I gain the greatest benefit as far as learning lessons that will help me in business."

"Where did you learn this?" Al asked. He was beginning to like Dave's perspective. "I mean I'm not lazy, don't get me wrong. But I like the idea of getting the most benefit for my work."

"And don't misunderstand me. I'm all for hard work. But I don't like working hard just for the sake of working hard. I want to work smarter, not just harder. To answer your question, no one specifically taught me what I'm telling you. I've learned it by observing, especially during my time as an undergraduate. Of course, you have to adjust what I'm saying to fit your own classes. Every course will be different, and you need to observe and find out what will provide you with the most learning and the highest grade reward for the time spent."

"In my literature course, we have to answer some home-work questions about each book we read," said Joanne. "But 90 percent of our grade comes from tests and quizzes, only 10 percent from the homework assignments."

"Let's analyze that. You don't want to ignore your home work, and doing it will probably help you prepare for the tests. Is that right?"

"Yes. But the students are complaining about the time it takes to do the homework. Most of us are spending an hour or more each night in addition to the reading."

"How do you think you can apply the 80/20 Rule here?"

"Well, maybe instead of devoting an hour to the homework, I can limit myself to 15 to 30 minutes. Then I could use more time to review my notes so I'm on top of the material for the next quiz."

"Good. You're getting the idea. Now while I was telling you about my business courses, I alluded to a second very important principle. Are you ready to write it down?"

"Ready, Mentor!" said Al, with pen poised in hand.

ALWAYS ATTEND CLASS

Al wrote the three words down, then looked up, obviously disappointed. "You've got to be kidding. That's a principle?"

"I said they were simple."

"I thought class attendance was assumed," said Joanne.

But Al protested. "You don't expect me to attend *every* class, do you? I don't mind math and science. But what about history? Dr. Sears is unbelievably boring."

"Let's discuss this principle for a minute. From my observation, there is a strong correlation between students who miss class and students who eventually drop out of school. The vast majority of classes are relevant to what the instructor expects you to learn. Think about it — attending class gives you thirty or more exposures to the subject. Repetition is crucial to learning. Furthermore, attending class is the best way to be sure you learn the particular lessons you're supposed to. It also helps you to know what the professor will put on the exam and require in the homework."

"Can't I just borrow someone's notes when I skip?" asked Al.

"You can, but there are some things you need to be doing in class that you won't pick up by reading someone else's notes. Which leads me to a third basic principle."

"Another index card?" asked Al.

"Right. I mentioned to you earlier about having objectives. You need to apply that to your classes. So write this down:

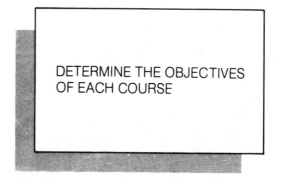

DETERMINE THE OBJECTIVES OF EACH COURSE

"Al, when you're on the basketball court, what's the team trying to do?"

"Score more points than the other team, of course."

"That's right. The objective is very clear. The biggest mistake students make is that they don't know what they're supposed to learn in their classes. That's one very important reason for you to attend class, because normally you won't pick up the objective by reading the textbook. Usually the professor reveals that in class. Knowing the objectives will tell you a lot about where to place your major emphasis in study.

"However, the professor doesn't always make the objective clear, and if he doesn't, you have to probe a little. That's where you could do yourself — and your classmates — a favor. Ask the professor to state the few essential things he wants you to get out of the course during the term."

"You mean we should ask that right in class?" said Al.

"You can do it in class or after class. Now that's not the only way to learn the objectives. You could also do it by asking someone who's taken the course previously. Or you could ask what's going to be on the final exam. The point is you need to learn the objectives during the first week. Do that and you're well on your way to becoming an 80/20 Student."

"What's an 80/20 Student?" asked Al.

"Is that someone who applies the 80/20 Rule?" asked Joanne.

"Right. An 80/20 Student has learned to work smarter, not just harder. He or she has learned those few crucial principles for success in school and diligently applies them. The 80/20 Student attends every class and learns the course objectives during the first week of class. Would you like to keep meeting to learn more about what an 80/20 Student does?"

"I'm game," said Al.

"So am I," said Joanne. "I can already see that a couple of hours with you might save me many hours later."

"Then let me give you an assignment."

"Oh no!" Al mocked.

"These principles work only if you put them into practice.

But I think you can handle that without any trouble. Between now and the next time we meet, attend every class. Also, find out the objective of each course and report back what you learn."

"I think I can handle that," said Al. A true athlete, he loved a challenge. He wanted to do well in school, and he knew he would do better if he had some coaching. The basketball coach always stressed fundamentals. So why shouldn't the same approach work with his studies?

Joanne was more reflective. She always attended class, but she'd never thought to ask about the objectives. "I appreciate your help," she said to Dave. "I'm already looking forward to next week."

3

LISTENING WITH
80/20 AGGRESSIVENESS

Al flopped down on the couch in the corner of the student union lounge. "Boy, did I make some points with Dr. Gordon this week!" he said.

Dave and Joanne seated themselves in two easy chairs opposite Al. "Tell us about it," said Dave.

"Well, it was in my engineering course. Dr. Gordon was explaining this long proof and all of us were writing it down. When he was done, he asked if there were any questions. I'm leaning back like this, see. . ." Al's legs were stretched out, amplifying his full 6'3" height, ". . .and I raise my hand. 'Dr. Gordon,' I say, real polite, 'could you explain where we're heading, exactly? What's the primary objective of the course? That would really help me understand what we've covered this week.'

" 'Well,' he said, 'sure, Al. That's a good question. The equation we've discussed this morning is one of four key equations you need to learn this term. If you want to get the guts of this course, learn these four equations and everything else we discuss will flow logically from that.' "

"Does knowing that help you in the class?" asked Dave.

"Are you kidding?" Al exclaimed "It's already made a huge difference. I know where we're going."

"That's a great report, Al. Joanne, how did you do?"

"Well, I didn't raise my hand in class. But in my English literature course, I went up to Professor McKenzie after class last Friday and asked what the course objective was. He said none of his students had ever asked him that before."

"Did he mind your asking?"

"He thought it was great. He told me that we'll be focusing primarily on the historical impact of the authors we study rather than the technical aspects of their writing."

"Do you feel that's going to help you?"

"It sure will! It's already helping me know what to look for when I read. One thing I plan to do is to write a one-page summary of the historical background for each book we study. I'm sure that will help me prepare for exams. Would you also like to hear what I learned about Bolger's class?"

"Sure."

"I talked with a girl who took the course last year. She said that the final exam stresses economic theory and that if I'd concentrate on the second section of the text — where the various theories of supply and demand are explained — the course will make a lot more sense."

"Terrific! You're both off to a great start. You'll soon be genuine 80/20 Students! You've already started observing how doing the right 20 percent of the activities well will yield 80 percent of the benefit. Did you notice you were learning any more in class as a result?"

"I did," volunteered Al.

Joanne was more specific. "After Dr. McKenzie told me that he was concentrating on the historical background of the literature, my mind seemed more alert during the next class period. Particularly when he talked about the political and religious influences on the life of John Milton, the writer we're studying right now."

"What you're discovering is the concept of aggressive thinking which starts with aggressive listening. Let's examine that a little more. Al, when your coach has something to tell you, what do you do?"

"When the coach talks, I listen," he said with a sober smile.

"Do you notice that you listen better in a particular position?"

"Position? What do you mean?"

"You said you like to lean way back and stretch out in class." Dave stretched out his legs to emphasize the point.

Then he pulled them back, leaned forward in his chair and stared intently at Al. "In which position do I appear more alert?"

"I see what you're getting at. You're right. When my coach is giving a chalk talk, I lean forward and hang on every word he says."

"That's one aspect of aggressive listening. Your body needs to get into it as well as your mind. You can listen in a relaxed position, but your your mind is more likely to wander."

"I see you've got some more cards for us," Joanne noted.

Dave handed them the cards. "I want you to write down the word SAFE as an acrostic. It will help you remember this concept." He jotted some words on a card, then showed it to them.

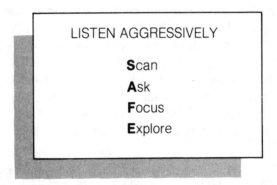

LISTEN AGGRESSIVELY

Scan

Ask

Focus

Explore

"Here's what's beginning to happen in class. *Scan* is the first word. The secret to aggressive listening is that your mind is like radar. You're alert, curious, aware of all that's being said and that's going on around you.

"Second is *Ask.* You should be constantly asking, 'Is this valuable? How does this fit the objective? Do I need to probe deeper?' For example, Joanne, after learning the objective in your literature class, you're more alert when the professor talks about historical background.

"Third is *Focus*. When you determine something is worth further attention, zero in on it.

"Last is *Explore*. Though we're talking about aggressive listening, here you may need to use your mouth, too. Ask questions to clarify a point. Examine and probe the topic carefully in order to gain full understanding.

"That's the concept; now you're wondering how it works. My two little boys illustrate it well. They play together all the time, and while they're chattering away, I'm aware of their voices, but I'm not really listening — just scanning. I'm somewhat aware of what they're doing while I concentrate on something else. Then suddenly something catches my attention. The other night Joshua said, 'No, John. No!' I didn't hear John respond and then Joshua yelled, 'No, John. No!' Something in his tone of voice told me there was a problem. Was John hurting Joshua? Or teasing him? It sounded like it was time for me to enter the picture.

"I began asking because of Joshua's words and the way his voice increased in volume. Then I focused by going into their room to see what was happening. And I explored by asking them some questions in order to find the cause of the problem and apply an appropriate solution. In this case, John had taken one of Joshua's favorite toys. I had to give the boys a little lesson about borrowing and sharing with each other."

Dave noticed that Al had his history notebook and asked to take a look at it. Al handed it over and Dave flipped through five pages that covered the lecture notes for the first five class sessions Al had already attended. "I notice after the third class, you wrote down the objectives. That's good. But here, two classes later, your page is blank."

Al shrugged his shoulders. "Yeah, well, nothing struck me. I've never been that good at taking notes."

Dave handed the notebook back to Al and asked Joanne for her literature notebook which was sitting on the top of her stack of books. The spiral-bound book was already one quarter full. "I see that for one class you have ten pages of notes," Dave commented.

Joanne accepted the observation as a compliment. She'd always been a voluminous note taker. Al stretched his neck out to look. "How can one human being write that much?" he wondered.

"Well, it's not easy," she admitted. "But if I go like crazy and don't think about anything else, I can get most of it down."

"I really commend your effort," Dave said, handing the notebook back to Joanne. "You really work at paying attention. And Al, I like the way you wrote the objectives down in big letters. It will be easy to refer back to them. But let's get back to the 80/20 Rule in relation to taking notes. Joanne, are all your notes of equal value?"

"Well, probably not. I'd have to go back through and decide."

"Do you think the 80/20 Rule would apply to what the professor says in class? In other words, in 20 percent of the class could the instructor be communicating the essence of 80 percent of the truth you need to learn? Those would be the most important points. Other parts of the class would support and add detail to those few essential truths."

"Maybe that's true. But how do you know what that 20 percent is?"

"Good question. I'd like to suggest you start using a new note-taking outline. It will help you focus on the 20 percent that will give you 80 percent of the benefit. You need to remember that you're engaged in a *learning* process. And that process will be maximized if you can spend at least some class time *involved* in what's being taught rather than just taking down information. Studies show that you are able to recall about eight times more of the content when you become involved than when you just listen. Twenty-four hours after a class, you will remember only about 10 percent of what you heard unless you repeat it, discuss it, apply it, or in other ways become aggressively involved in cementing the material in your memory.

Dave took a yellow pad from his briefcase and on the first sheet, about three quarters of the way down, he drew a line across the page. Then he divided that quarter into three sections. He wrote some words in each section and showed the paper to Joanne and Al.

80/20 NOTES (**S**can/**A**sk)		
80/20 REACTIONS (**F**ocus)	80/20 QUESTIONS (**E**xplore)	80/20 LESSONS (Summarize)

"Here's how you can use the SAFE approach when taking notes," Dave said. "The longest part of the page is for 80/20 Notes. This is where you write important points learned from *Scanning* and *Asking*. Scanning means you're listening alertly to what the professor says. But you don't write everything down, because not all that he or she says is of equal value. You're constantly asking which 20 percent is most important. That's the second step in SAFE. You do the asking by looking and listening for clues that the professor gives. For example, if the professor says that something is 'key,' or 'major,' or 'important,' bells should go off in your head. This is worth noting. You'll want to write that down in the note section. If he says something like, 'now it's interesting to note,' or 'parenthetically,' or 'some people explain it this way,' those comments usually indicate side roads, not main points."

"Dr. McKenzie likes to do that," Joanne said. "He said he's not emphasizing the technical aspects of literature, but he often makes technical observations. He'll also mention various opinions about an influence in a writer's life before stating a synthesis of all these influences."

"Good example. If you know that his primary objective is to explore the historical influences, then you don't want to ignore those other points, but you don't focus on them either. Let me also add that there are usually nonverbal clues to help you know what the teacher considers important. He may stand a little straighter. Or she may look up from her notes and speak from the heart. Listen for voice inflection, or watch for when he writes a little harder or more aggressively on the blackboard. Those are often signals that the professor considers this an important point. That's where you want to take note and focus."

Dave emphasized that it wasn't necessary to write down every word on subpoints. "You're looking for the primary points of the professor's outline. Then when he illustrates those points or makes supportive observations, you might just jot down several words or a sentence that will jog your memory later. You're constantly trying to learn the main points and observe how the professor is accomplishing the main objectives of the class. If you find that the professor requires you to note a lot of detail, then at least flag particularly crucial points with arrows or asterisks so you can see them clearly."

Dave asked for Joanne's notebook again. He showed her that in several cases she'd written part of a quotation from the book being discussed. "Probably all you need to do is write down the page that is being quoted from. You can go back to it later. And Al, if Dr. Gordon is giving a proof and it's in the book, is it necessary to write it down?"

"I guess not."

"Now don't just daydream with the spare time. We've said that class time is precious. So use the opportunity to listen to the professor's line of reasoning. Interact with her in your mind, so you're learning. Maybe you need to make note of a critical point in the development of the proof."

"So you're saying you focus on what the teacher emphasizes," said Joanne.

"Right. You're constantly asking, 'How does this fit the objective?' 'Do I need to focus on this?' You see, if all you needed was the textbook, it would be simple. Why do we have class, anyway?"

"Because things need to be explained," said Joanne.

"That's right. So you don't want to write a second text. The goal is comprehension. That doesn't mean everything will fit on one page. Sometimes you'll need to take down a lot of important information that you won't get from any other place than in class. But that will be unusual in most courses. In fact, if you do miss something important, there's usually at least one prolific note taker in every class, and you can probably retrieve that information. But that situation will be rare.

"Now if you're not furiously writing everything down, what do you do with the extra time? That's where these three columns at the bottom of the page come in. The first one, the 80/20 Reactions column, is where you internalize — it's the focus part of our SAFE acrostic. You may tie something the instructor says to something you have read in the textbook. You may note how it fits with the course objective. You may see patterns emerging from several points the professor has made. By the way, this is a crucial point in the learning process. You want to do more than learn facts; you want to see connections between those facts. The key here is that you're actively learning, not simply taking down information."

Al noted the next box read "80/20 Questions."

"That's right. This is where you are doing the exploring in the SAFE outline. As you're making notes and reacting, you want to generate some questions and have them ready to roll, either in class or after class."

"What if I don't have any questions?" asked Joanne.

"I find that I can usually generate a question in one of three areas. Here is where you become very aggressive in learning. In fact, I think this is worth a three-by-five card:

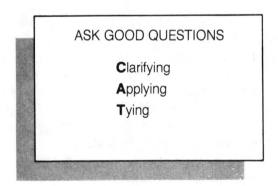

ASK GOOD QUESTIONS

Clarifying

Applying

Tying

"CAT! That's easy to remember," laughed Joanne.

"Right! The *C* stands for *Clarifying* questions. That's where I'm trying to understand exactly what the professor means. *Applying* takes it one step further. I want to know how this works in real life. I might ask how it works in his or her experience, or I might ask how I can apply what has been taught.

"Finally, *Tying* is a very important kind of question, for that helps us make linkages with what we already know. You might ask how the material just covered relates to something the professor taught the previous week, or to the course objectives. Or you might compare the information with your previous education on the subject; that would be particularly helpful in your major field."

"The last column of this outline is '80/20 Lessons,' " noted Joanne. "Does that mean I make a statement about what's been covered during the class period?"

"Yes. Near the close of the period, or as soon as class ends, try to write a one-sentence summary of the class session. What is the main point? What is the most important thing to remember? You'll find this box very valuable when you prepare for exams. Just thumbing through the summary statements will often provide a concise review of the course."

"I suppose using this outline is our homework assignment," said Al.

"Yes, I'd like you to try this note-taking outline for the next week. Al, I think it will help you know what to put in your notes. And Joanne, remember this: Don't be a scribe; be a thinker. I think you'll find that one or two pages of notes yields more results than ten pages of transcription."

"I'll be an 80/20 Student!" Al and Dave laughed at Joanne's comment. They all stood to go their separate ways. "I'm already feeling smarter," she added.

"That's right!" said Dave. "That could almost be our motto. Work smarter, not harder. Next week, we'll talk about how to make use of those notes during class. See you then."

4

PRESENTING
WITH 80/20 IMPACT

Al and Joanne eagerly put their new note-taking outlines to use. In engineering class, Al found himself following the line of reasoning better because he didn't have to focus on getting every line of every proof on paper. Often he had his textbook open to the proof and jotted an occasional note in the book when Dr. Gordon made an important point.

History was more difficult for Al. His reaction and question boxes were usually blank. But the summary box was a major help. He always made sure that was filled at the end of class, and he reviewed the previous day's summary statement right before the next class started in order to be mentally alert for the lecture.

Joanne found herself enjoying classes more when she didn't have to take down every word that was spoken. Arrows and asterisks helped her recognize main points. She often wrote reactions in light of the course objectives and inevitably developed three or four questions during the process.

Dave praised the progress of his students as they met at a popular off-campus coffee shop. "As with anything new, this will take some practice," he said to encourage Al.

"I guess it feels a little awkward. It's simpler just to take down the facts and think about them later."

"I understand your feeling. But let me ask you something. When your basketball coach gives you a new play, how long does it take until you're comfortable with it?"

"Well, we practice every play many times. Sometimes I get it right away. Usually, though, it takes a fair amount of repetition. Last year, coach put in a new trapping zone press.

It took most of the season before the team was effective with it."

"If it was so hard, why didn't you just stick with the other defenses you had used? Judging by the team's record, you were pretty effective without the press."

"Yes, but once we mastered it, we were even tougher. I think that's why we all hung in there; Coach convinced us it would work and we believed him."

"Do you believe this note-taking system will work?"

"I guess so. For one thing, it's helping me learn more in class. Don't worry, I'll get it before long."

Joanne was concerned about the "80/20 Questions" column. "I have no problem coming up with questions. But I've never been one to talk in class. I'd rather let the other students ask the questions."

"Okay, put yourself in the professor's shoes for a minute. You come into the classroom and what do you see?"

"In history, I'd see forty sleeping students," said Al.

"What does that do to you as a professor?"

"Doesn't make me too excited about teaching."

"So what students will you tend to appreciate? Will anyone have an advantage?"

Joanne was beginning to see Dave's train of thought. "I'd be pleased if a student were dressed neatly, sitting up straight, wide awake, pencil and paper in hand — ready to go."

"Good. Al, can you think of anything else?"

"Well, if a student consistently asks good questions or makes astute — I like that word — astute observations. I think that would tell me the person was paying attention."

"Suppose a student sits there and never says anything."

Al laughed. "I'd probably figure he's thinking about his date for next Saturday night."

"It's time for another index card."

Al and Joanne sat up straight, poised and ready. They suddenly realized what they were doing and all three laughed. "You're definitely prize students!" said Dave. "Here's what I want you to write:

> IT'S NOT JUST WHAT YOU
> KNOW BUT WHAT YOU SHOW

"The point is simple: You don't get graded on what's in your head. Your grade comes from what you show the professor. So you need a high *Show-to-Know* ratio. Now what are the ways you can show the professor what you know?"

"Exams," said Joanne. "And homework."

"That's two. There's one more."

Al and Joanne looked at each other, then back to Dave.

"It gets back to what the professor is looking for in the students."

"Oh, what you say in class," said Joanne.

"Right! If you never say anything in class, the professor can't tell what you're thinking."

"I'm in one class with two hundred other students," said Al. "It's straight lecture."

"So you can't apply it there. However, does that class have some sort of discussion group format?"

"We meet once a week in groups of fifteen with a graduate assistant."

"Then that's where you apply the principle. In fact, does that graduate assistant do the grading?"

"I think so."

"So there's your chance to show what you know."

Joanne noted that there was one student in her economics

class who always talked and was obnoxious about it.

"That's a good point," Dave agreed. "You certainly can talk *too* much. It's not so much quantity as quality. Remember the 80/20 Student. She wants to get the maximum benefit when she does talk. Your new way of taking notes will help you do that."

"I don't think I understand," said Joanne. "I see now that I should speak up, but when, and how?"

"Remember last week when I mentioned three kinds of questions?" Dave asked.

"Yes. CAT! *Clarifying, Applying* and *Tying.*"

"Let me give you an example of how I used applying last week. One of my instructors was telling us the importance of supervisors communicating to their employees that they care about them. A little later, she observed that our body language, tone of voice, and choice of words may communicate the exact opposite message. The dilemma is that our real attitudes are eventually expressed by involuntary communication.

"Well, I asked if a reasonable application would be for us to work at having the right attitudes, which would then work their way out so that we would communicate the right things verbally *and* through our body language, tone of voice, and so on. The instructor said yes and elaborated on how important right attitudes are.

"There's something else I could have done. I could have asked her to illustrate the concept from her experience. I'd have said something like, 'Professor Smith, from your experience consulting with many companies, could you give an illustration of an employer who said the right words but communicated the wrong message?' That's a very effective kind of question, for it helps clarify the concept and also demonstrates application."

"It seems that it's pretty important just how you phrase a question or statement," observed Joanne.

"Very much so," Dave acknowledged. "In fact, before you convey what you're going to say in class, you really need to take three things into account."

"Another three-by-five card, Mentor?" asked Al.

"Another three-by-five card. I kind of like that term 'Mentor.' Sounds very dignified. Here are the three points:

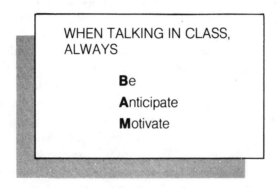

WHEN TALKING IN CLASS,
ALWAYS

Be

Anticipate

Motivate

"Do you notice what word this acrostic spells?"

"BAM!" laughed Al. "That's a word with impact — just what we want to have in class, right?"

"You've got it! Let's take each one separately. First, *Be.* That means be someone people will listen to. Just how important are first impressions?"

"Depends on the situation," said Al.

"To a professor?"

"Probably pretty important."

"I agree. Unless it's a small class, the professor probably won't have much individual contact with you. So appearance — even how you dress, attentiveness in class, the way you present yourself — those things are significant."

Joanne mentioned that one of her professors looked especially tired the other day. "I guess we really need to remember that our instructors are people, too. Do you think it's okay to say something?"

"Like what?"

"Oh, ask if everything is okay. Or mention that I appreciated the lecture."

"If that's natural for you, then yes. That's a good idea."

"Couldn't it be considered manipulative?" asked Al.

"I'd be careful. But if you genuinely care, then go ahead. In fact, that was my point about body language. If our heart attitude is right, then our words and actions will reflect that. So if you are genuinely concerned, I wouldn't worry about it being misconstrued. To be honest with you, I didn't always have the right attitude and it really did affect my relationships in a negative way. But something very dramatic happened in my life to change that. I'll tell you about it later."

"The second element of talking in class is *Anticipate.* That's planning, thinking through what you're going to say before you say it. Your note-taking outline helps you a lot right there. Use it to think through how you're going to phrase a question. Sometimes I make an observation that leads into the question. But be careful you don't ramble."

"One time I couldn't get recognized in class because so many others wanted to talk," said Al. "I wrote down my thoughts so I wouldn't forget them. One of the side benefits was that when my chance finally came, I was well organized."

"That's right," Dave said. "You made a better presentation. Can you explain why?"

"Because I planned it, rather than speaking off the top of my head."

"Then let's take this principle and use it to our advantage all the time." Dave laughed as he suddenly remembered an experience in one of his business courses that illustrated the unexpected benefits of being prepared and talking in class. "It was a case study. Professor Jackson was getting frustrated because no one was coming up with what he considered the right answer.

The case had to do with selling dog food. As another student was talking, I suddenly thought of the word 'gatekeeper.' I jotted it down on my notes, in the box labeled 'questions.' Then I mentally prepared an introductory state-ment that it doesn't matter whether the dog thinks it's the greatest dog food, but that the people *think* dogs think it's the greatest dog food. That led to my question, 'Aren't we dealing with the gatekeeper concept here? People make the decision, and therefore aren't they in effect the gatekeepers or controllers of what the dogs will eat?' When I finally was able to ask my question, Dr. Jackson got real excited. You'd have thought I'd discovered the idea of the century. Talk about scoring high in class."

"And if you hadn't said anything, you'd have lost on that opportunity to show what you knew," observed Joanne.

"That's right."

"What does it mean to *Motivate?*" Joanne asked, looking at her card again.

"That's the *way* you communicate," Dave responded. "You want to be as interesting and persuasive as possible. You want to present a strong case, which includes making a strong opening to get people's attention. You want to make eye contact with the professor, if possible. Depending on the personality of the speaker, there are many ways to communicate. Enthusiasm. Demonstrating interest. Being authentic. For some, a good way to communicate is through humor."

"That's Al!" said Joanne with a smile.

"She's right, Al. You can use your sense of humor to an advantage. Humor helps people relax, and that makes it easier to learn. Just be careful you don't poke fun at the professor."

"Except for Dr. Jones. We're always kidding each other."

"I'm not a good joke teller," said Joanne.

"But you have other strengths. You're obviously sincere. You care deeply about things. That can come out when you speak."

"Do I read my questions off the page? It seems hard to be sincere when you're reading."

"I think it's better to be spontaneous. You've prepared by writing down your thoughts. Now look up and say it from your heart. I'd rather risk missing a point and appear spontaneous. But don't do like some people who are very spontaneous and have no content. You must have something worth saying."

"Time has flown," said Joanne. "I've got to be at work in half an hour."

"We're done," Dave said. "Your assignment is to say something in class. Look for an opportunity to ask a question or make an observation. Next week we'll compare notes on how it goes."

5

DOING
HOMEWORK RIGHT

It was a cold and damp fall afternoon that called for something hot to drink. Joanne and Dave were both a few minutes early. They noticed the corner tables were occupied and settled for one in the middle of the busy coffee shop.

Dave asked Joanne about her week. "It's hard for me to speak up in class," she said, wrapping her hands around her cup of hot chocolate. "I have no problem coming up with good questions. But the first time I had a chance to talk, I chickened out. I finally got up enough courage on Monday — in economics. It's easy to think of clarifying questions there; Bolger's hard to follow."

"How did it go?"

"Dr. Bolger thought I had a good question. So that was a positive response. I felt pretty good after it was over. Then I asked a question the next day in my lit class. That's a little easier because I'm more comfortable with the subject matter."

"You're doing very well. Talking in class is definitely easier for some students than others. But with practice you can at least become comfortable with the process. Remember what I told Al about practicing his basketball plays last week?"

Joanne nodded. "I'll keep working at it."

Al finally arrived, soaked from riding his bike across campus in the rain. Grabbing a cup of coffee and a piece of pecan pie he joined Dave and Joanne.

"People are taking notice!" Al said, his eyes showing excitement. "One guy came up to me after class yesterday. 'You've changed,' he told me. 'I didn't think you were so smart.' "

"He noticed you were participating more in class?" asked Joanne.

"Yeah, it was great. He wanted to know what had happened to me. I said I'd be glad to get together with him sometime and tell him about it."

"I like that," said Dave. "You learn more when you have to teach."

"How's that?"

"Well, take our time together, for instance. I'm learning more about studying as I teach you what I've learned. It reminds me to practice the basics in my own classes. Teaching is a great way to clarify your thinking. When I was at State Tech, I tutored, and inevitably it helped me in my own studies."

Joanne was quiet, staring into her cup of tea. Dave asked if something was bothering her. "I'm buried," she admitted. "I've gotten way behind on my reading."

"The twenty-five books you have to read?"

"I like to keep up with the reading so I can follow McKenzie's lectures. I'm about three classes behind now."

"That's no big deal," laughed Al. "I'm a week behind on my homework for all but one of my classes. That's normal."

"Well, that's not unusual, but it may not be the best way," said Dave.

"Are you going to tell us that one of your principles is to do everything on time?"

"That's not a bad idea. But I understand that students get behind. I could preach against, it but it probably wouldn't make much difference. I do have another principle." He handed them more index cards.

ALWAYS TURN IN YOUR
HOMEWORK

"That's pretty basic," said Al.

"Let's take your engineering class, for example. Is most of the homework problem solving?"

Al nodded.

"And how much of your grade depends on those assignments?"

"Quite a bit. As much as 50 percent if you do the extra-credit problems."

"Okay, then even if you don't solve every problem well, hand in what you've done. Of course, do the best you can. But remember that partial credit always beats no credit. That's the *Show-to-Know* principle. Homework is one of only three ways you can show the professor what you know. Also, remember that other students are probably struggling, too; everyone's got a lot to do. And most courses are graded on somewhat of a curve. So don't keep turning in your homework late all the time because of your perfectionism.

"Now let's talk about some principles. There really are three most common types of homework — reading, writing, and problem solving. Sometimes there are practice-and-development-of-skills homework assignments — such as for music and art classes. But let's practice the 80/20 Rule and concentrate on helping you with the three most common types. Since Joanne is behind in reading, let's focus on that today. Joanne, perhaps you can tell me how you read a book?"

Joanne looked puzzled. "What do you mean?"

"When do you read?"

"Whenever I can. But usually at night."

"And where do you read?"

"In the dorm, primarily in my room."

"And what is going on around you as you read."

"Well, my roommate usually has the TV on. There's quite a bit of noise on my floor."

"Is the television distracting?"

"Sometimes. If there's a show on that I like, it's hard to concentrate on my reading."

"Do you enjoy reading?"

"I do, especially fiction. I get quite involved in the novels."

"How about you, Al? You have to do some reading, don't you?"

"Mostly for history class. It's the most boring textbook ever written."

"How do you read?"

"I like to get as comfortable as possible. I stretch out on my bed, prop the pillow behind me, put on the headphones and listen to some good music. The only problem is that two pages and I'm asleep. The text is that boring."

"Okay, let's analyze your situations. Joanne, when are you most alert? Are you a morning or an evening person?"

"Definitely evening. My brain doesn't start functioning until ten in the morning."

"What about you, Al?"

"Well, with basketball practice, I'm often very tired in the evening. I'm probably most alert in the morning."

"Here's our second card for today. This is a good general principle that applies in every area, not just homework:

MAKE THE MOST OF YOUR
STRENGTHS

"Let me illustrate. There are two facts about me that I use to my advantage. First, I am a morning person. After nine at night, I'm gone. So I study in the morning. Often I'm up at four or five. It's very quiet, and I get far more done than if I tried to work until midnight."

"I didn't know anyone studied at five in the morning," observed Al.

"Why not?" Dave asked. "Just because others don't doesn't mean you can't. There are certain times of the day when we're significantly more efficient. Those are the times when we're really clicking and we probably get four or five times more done than when we're tired or there's a lot of distraction."

"You're right. Sometimes late at night I have to reread something four or five times. My eyes pass over the page but I'm not really absorbing the content."

"And the point is to absorb the content and link it to the objectives of the course and the other material you're learning. If you don't achieve that, you're really wasting your time. If in the morning, or some other time, you can focus and absorb material the first time through, then you're clearly applying the 80/20 Rule. Apply the right 20 percent of your time, the time when you're really focused, and that probably equals what you'd do the other 80 percent of your time when you might not be as focused on the subject."

"That makes a lot of sense," Al agreed. "I guess the only thing that bothers me is that when I work at night, it's open-ended. In the morning, I have a time limit. I have to go to class."

"That's true. But you may also find that because of the time limit, you use your time more efficiently. Plus I find that that factor helps me prepare for exams, which are time periods with definite ending points. It's good to practice thinking about a subject under a certain amount of pressure."

"I guess it's worth a try."

"Here's the second fact about myself," Dave continued. "I work better standing up than sitting down. And Al, I certainly can't work lying down. At my company office, I have a stand-up desk with a huge surface on which I can spread things out, and I work all day long on my feet. I have a similar desk in my study at home."

"You're saying do what works best for you, regardless of what everyone else is doing," said Joanne.

"That's correct. Joanne, you're probably studying at the right time. Your problem is that you're distracted."

"I've always had a lot of noise around when I studied. At home there were five kids. The TV was always on. I shared a room with my sister and she played the stereo all the time."

"What happens when you're in a quiet place? Do you study better?"

"It depends. If it's noisy, say the TV is on but it's not something that interests me, then I'm okay. But if I'm being distracted, it's definitely better to move to a quiet place. At home I couldn't completely block out the noise, but sometimes I did study in the kitchen."

"So you may want to find a new study spot, some place where you can get away when it's too noisy. Maybe the library. Or a quiet corner in the student union. This is a very important principle: Understand and use your strengths when you study.

"Now let's talk about how to read. Joanne, you said you

get emotionally involved in the novels?"

"Yes, I think that's why I started reading in the first place. I really enjoy living in the worlds that writers can create."

"I'd like you to be able to enjoy every book to the limit," Dave said. "I really would. But let me ask you, if you did that, would you get all those books read plus the work you need to do for your other classes?"

"No, that's my problem."

"Do you enjoy that situation?"

"No, I'm frustrated. It's hard to enjoy reading these books when I'm so far behind."

"Then let's talk about how we can speed up the process. I want you to be able to enjoy your reading, indeed, all of your school experience. That's one of the reasons for our meeting together. But trying to live every detail of every book is actually hindering you right now. So let me make a suggestion. Would you agree that probably 80 percent of the benefit from your reading will come from 20 percent of the content?"

"I'm not sure about that."

"Do you have to know every detail of every book when you take your tests?"

"No. But how do you know which part to concentrate on? I mean, everything's tied together."

"That's true. But when you're reading a novel, aren't there usually a few main characters and then a number of lesser characters? There's usually a main plot and some sub-plots. There is one main theme plus some other interesting but perhaps not crucial points along the way."

"I'm following you."

"My point is that there may be a lot of material that's worth only skimming," Dave noted. "Only some is worth actually studying."

"Judging from what the professor emphasizes in class, you're probably right."

"Then let's see if we can figure a way to help you think aggressively and glean the 20 percent that will give you 80 percent of the benefit. What was the word we used for aggressive listening two weeks ago?"

"SAFE!" said Al, spreading his hands out flat like a baseball umpire.

"You're crazy!" said Joanne with a laugh. Al certainly kept things from getting too serious.

"Let's see how it applies to reading," Dave said.

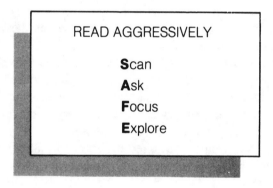

READ AGGRESSIVELY

Scan

Ask

Focus

Explore

"It starts with *Scan.* Isn't it helpful to get the big picture of a book first before you absorb too many details? What would be some ways to learn what your book is about before you start reading it line by line?"

Joanne thought for a moment. "Well, one way is to read the copy on the back cover."

"Good. What else?"

"Sometimes the table of contents is helpful. But some novels don't have them; the chapters are just numbered."

"What about an introduction?"

"Yes, some of my books have an introduction that tells a little about the author, the book, the historical setting."

"So that would give you some overview, a context. Here's another idea. You might read the first and last paragraphs of each chapter; you might even skim what seem to be a couple of key chapters. What you are looking for is the overall theme of the book, the main point the author is making."

Dave told how he occasionally enjoys reading certain popular novels for relaxation. "Last weekend, I picked up a paperback novel that intrigued me. It's supposed to be a fairly accurate account of the inner workings of a major daily newspaper. It was 375 pages and I read it in four hours because there were quite a few extraneous things that didn't interest me. I skimmed right over them and concentrated on the parts I found most interesting. You can do the same thing with the books you have to read."

"Do you think it would help to take a speed reading course?"

"Definitely, especially with your major. I can give you some principles to get you started, but by all means take a speed reading course as soon as you can. After all, how many hours do you spend reading each evening?"

"At least three," Joanne stated.

"Just think, if you could cut that by half — how much more time you would have available for other things," Dave said with excitement. "Besides, it's been established that comprehension actually improves with some increase in reading speed. So that's an additional benefit. However, let's see what we can do to help improve your speed right away with the SAFE outline.

"The second step is *Ask.* As you start reading the book — and now you're reading as fast as you can, skimming — ask yourself 'What's important? How does this chapter relate to the overall purpose of the book? Is this incident a side road the author is taking or central to the plot or thesis? Is this character important, or is he just making a cameo appearance?'

"While you read, have a pen in your hand. You buy all your books, don't you?"

"Some I get new, some used from the book exchange. But I like to keep them so I can underline."

"Underlining slows you down," Dave asserted. "I suggest you put marks in the margins."

"Sounds like I'm starting to *Focus*." said Joanne.

"Yes, exactly. Put an asterisk or arrow by key points. You might write down numbers to help you remember the sequence of events. Since your professor is focusing on historical influence, you might put an "H" by things that demonstrate a writer's historical perspective. Now you're determining what's worth your attention. You're becoming more aggressive, attacking the subject, analyzing it. You're concentrating on the portions that will yield the greatest benefit to your understanding in class, in papers, and on exams."

"What about *Explore?*"

"Remember when you said you were going to write a one-page synopsis of the historical background for each book? That's one way to explore — by looking for information beyond the book. Explore may also involve you in breaking down and analyzing a few critical passages. For example, you might take a character and see how he or she compares to an historical person of that era. You might explore by looking up a few key words in an encyclopaedia or dictionary. Or by developing some questions for class."

"Or maybe by looking up some background information in the library?" she asked.

"Right. Because you're not burdened with having to absorb every word of a book, you can zero in on the most important elements and gain greater understanding of them."

"What you say makes sense," Joanne agreed. "Much as I enjoy getting into a book, I'm going to enjoy more keeping up with my class assignments."

"Let's try a little experiment," Dave suggested. "Between now and next week, keep track of how many pages you read an hour. Compare that number to what you're covering right now."

"What's my assignment?" asked Al.

"I'd like you to try and adjust your schedule. See if you can go to bed earlier and do some of your studying in the morning when you're most alert.

"Now here's a bonus tip," Dave continued. "I promised that you would have more fun, and here's one way to do that. Set a goal of reading a certain amount or completing a certain number of problems. When you've accomplished it, reward yourself by taking a break and doing something you enjoy. When I finish an assignment, I might take a coffee break, read the newspaper, play with the kids, or take a walk.

"Think of some things you'd like to do and make them incentives, things to enjoy when you've reached a goal. Maybe you'll talk to a friend or listen to some music. The breaks don't have to be long. Usually ten or fifteen minutes is all I need before I'm ready to hit the books again."

Joanne and Al said they would follow Dave's suggestions. It was frustrating to get behind, and they both wanted to catch up in their classes. So they were eager to see just how well the 80/20 techniques would work.

6

WRITING 80/20 PAPERS

Joanne raved about the results of her week. She had completely caught up with her reading, something she had not expected. It didn't hurt that another class was cancelled one day, giving her an unexpected block of extra time which she used to good advantage. She was surprised to discover that she had nearly doubled the number of pages covered each hour because she was skimming certain sections. However, comprehension was not being sacrificed. She'd scored 100 percent on two consecutive pop quizzes for the first time.

Al was pleased with his new schedule as well, though he had had to buy a pair of earplugs in order to get to sleep at 10 p.m. Most students in the dorm were still up then, playing stereos, watching television, or fooling around. He tried not to disturb his roommate when he rose at five in the morning. A couple of mornings he slept until six. Still he accomplished far more at that time of day than he used to in the evening; the history reading went quickly and his mind was more alert when he worked on engineering problems.

Al leaned forward and flipped through one of the popular magazines that lay on the coffee tables in the student lounge. "I have a history paper due in three days," he said, without his normal jovial spirit. "I hate doing papers, so usually I wait until the last minute. Probably not what an 80/20 Student should do, right?"

Dave didn't answer the question but tossed it back to Al. "Why don't you think an 80/20 Student should wait to write a paper?"

"Well, the results aren't that good. You said the professor can only grade on what you show. If I wait till the last minute, chances are it won't be my best work."

"When do you usually write your papers?"

"The night before. However, I have gathered some ideas by then."

"Let's analyze what's happening. You told me last week that you're most alert in the morning. So you're making a fundamental mismatch of your best creative time when you write your papers at night. Think about how you are presenting yourself to the professor."

"I get the message. I've got to start sooner."

"There are several other reasons why you shouldn't wait until the last minute. Can you think of them?"

Al couldn't think of anything, so Dave prodded him: "You've just started basketball season, haven't you?"

"Yes. Last year, I waited until the last minute on one paper and I had forgotten about a road game the JV team had. I didn't get home until midnight. That paper was late and the prof marked me down one grade. Got a *D.*"

"So that's another reason," Dave noted. "If you wait too long, you may have scheduling conflicts. Another reason is that you're not allowing what I call 'soak time.' You're not maximizing the use of your mind. Your subconscious can do a lot of work for you *if* you give it time."

"I don't like the worry when I wait until the last minute," said Joanne.

"That's a good point. Worry is bad. It robs you of valuable energy that can be used in more productive ways. Sometime soon I will explain more about how you can deal with worry.

"Al, we can't completely make up for lost time, but here are some things that will help in the future. I have to write a paper a week for one class. I use the same concept in business when I have to write reports. It's called the standard paper schedule. I write in my schedule book the latest date I can begin working on a paper and still have a good finished product. I know what that date is by looking at the natural schedule of any paper or report."

Dave wrote out a schedule on a three-by-five card:

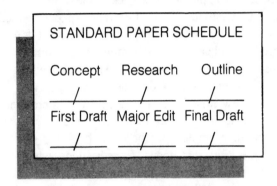

STANDARD PAPER SCHEDULE

Concept   Research   Outline
___/___   ___/___   ___/___
First Draft Major Edit Final Draft
___/___   ___/___   ___/___

"I work backwards. First I write down the due date under 'Final Draft.' Usually the final draft is typed the day before. In order to have that ready, the first draft has to be completed another day earlier so there's time to rewrite and polish, and so on. The date I put down for concept is the latest date I can afford to start.

"Let me give an example. For my management class, I have to write a paper each week. It's not too long, no more than five pages. And it's due every Friday. I have to start the concept stage no later than Monday evening. Tuesday, I review the research and outline the paper. That all goes in a file folder which I review right before I go to bed Tuesday night. That allows time for my subconscious to work. I type the first draft Wednesday morning before I leave for campus. I do my major editing on Thursday and type the final copy on Friday morning."

"My paper has to be eight to ten pages," said Al. "I've checked some books out of the library, but I haven't looked at them."

"Let's talk about the process," Dave encouraged. "Do you remember the outline for talking in class?"

"Let me think. BAM. *Be, Anticipate* and *Motivate.*"

"Good. Let's use the same outline for writing a paper."

"How can you *Be* in a paper?" asked Al.

"Why don't you put yourself back in the professor's shoes?"

Joanne understood. "First, I'd want a paper handed in on time. Second, I'd want it to be neat. Third, I'd want it to be interesting, clear and understandable in format."

"Those are excellent points," Dave acknowledged. "Remember first impressions do count. A paper that is typed neatly with few mistakes leaves a positive impression. I was a grader my senior year at Tech. One student submitted his final exam in a stapled notebook of half-size sheets — the spiral-bound kind that leave frayed edges when you tear them out. It was narrow-lined paper and he wrote with a fat, felt-tip pen. When he ran out of space, he continued writing up the sides of the paper. It was a mess! And reading it was really hard. He had good material, but it was difficult to look past the appearance to give him a decent grade."

Dave suggested that Al and Joanne write the following on a card:

WHEN WRITING PAPERS

Be: Neatness/Clarity

Anticipate: Objective/Outline/
Illustrations

Motivate: Lead/Enthusiasm/
People/Close

"That's a lot to remember," said Al.

"It will make more sense as we go through it. You'll notice I added *clarity* to *Be.* I think it's important to be well organized, so it's easy to follow your train of thought. One thing I often do is use subheads to divide each major section of the paper.

"Under *Anticipate,* we're talking about planning. I suggest that you start a file for each paper. When Wednesday morning rolls around, I'm ready to go on the paper because it's all in my file. The first thing that goes in there is the *objective.*"

"Sounds familiar," said Joanne, who was taking notes.

"Always determine the objective," Dave advised. "When you don't do that, how do you know what to put in the paper? Second, is *outline.*"

"Do you always have an outline before you start writing?" asked Joanne.

"Yes. Of course, the outline sometimes changes when I begin writing. What I do is write my ideas on index cards, usually as I'm doing my research, and put them in the file. Before I write, I spread those cards out on my desk, looking for a logical sequence of ideas. Once I organize those cards, I have my outline."

Al wanted to know what *illustrations* meant.

"As you're reading your books and you find a good quote that goes with a point in your outline, that's an illustration. Jot down the name of the book, the page number and a two- or three-word description. Other forms of illustration are facts, anecdotes, jokes. . ."

"You put jokes in your papers?" Al asked Dave eagerly.

"Sometimes, though I do it more when I speak. But if I can use humor and make a point in the process, I will. Actually this leads right into motivation. Remember that people are both rational and emotional beings. If you want to motivate someone — and you do want to motivate your professor, he or she is your reader — you need to tug at the emotions. Humor is one of the best ways to do that. One professor I love rarely goes five minutes without laughter in his class. He once told me, 'I open their mouths with laughter and while they are open, I feed them a point.' I've read a couple of his books and he does the same thing with his writing."

Dave pointed to Joanne's books. "Joanne, do you find it easier to read some books than others?"

"Yes, there are some books I'd never read unless I had to. And there are a couple of books I've started for my own enjoyment, but I never got past the first couple of chapters because I found they didn't interest me."

"Suppose you were the grader for a big stack of history papers. What kind of paper would stand out?"

"Well, it would have to be interesting. If all a student did was list facts and figures, I'd get bored. I would want to know what those facts meant. I guess I'd want to be emotionally involved."

"Excellent," said Dave. "Why bore the reader if it's not necessary? Convey the information that needs to be communicated and also make your writing fresh and interesting. Then it stands to reason that the instructor will enjoy reading the paper more, see how much more you have learned, and possibly give you a better grade.

"The *Motivate* section gives you some ideas as to how to do that. First, you need a good start, or what's called a *lead* in journalism."

"This is discouraging," said Al. "I don't think I can do all this."

"It's easier than you think if you've done a good job of planning. You've got those cards in your file. Sort them, looking for a good lead, a good *close*, and one or more illustrations for each point."

"Gotcha. Now about *enthusiasm*. How do you get that in a history paper?"

"You don't enjoy history, do you, Al?"

"No, I really don't."

"That probably shows in your writing. But try to put some excitement on paper. One way to do that is to express things in positive terms. Another is to have a quick pace. And change the format occasionally. Don't just make a point, cite a quote, make another point, cite another quote. Put some variety in the form."

"Why do you have the word *people* under *Motivate?*"
asked Al.

"Who lived out history?" Dave countered.

"People, of course."

"That's right. History isn't just dates, and names, and
locations, and wars. Think about it; you probably enjoy
reading about people." Dave picked up a copy of *Reader's
Digest* from the coffee table and held it out to them. "Do
you ever read this magazine?"

"Sure, but what has that got to do with term papers?"

"Do you realize that more than 31 million copies of
Reader's Digest are sold each month? Why do you think it's
the most popular magazine in the world?"

"It's easy to read. Enjoyable."

"Did you know that every single article talks about people?"

"Wait a minute; let me see that." Al grabbed the magazine
and looked at the table of contents on the cover. "Here's an
article about gardens. That's not about people." He handed
the magazine back to Dave.

"I'll bet it is!" Dave turned to the article. "Second paragraph, it talks about a Gallup survey of home gardeners.
Third paragraph discusses how gardeners feel about their
gardens, and gives a quote: 'Have you ever had a really
fresh turnip? Tastes just like an apple.' The next paragraph
talks about home-grown tomatoes and quotes the editor of
Sunset magazine." Dave turned the page. "Here's a paragraph
about bugs. And it talks about how gardeners deal with
them. I could keep going, but do you get the point?"

"Maybe you were lucky." Al took the magazine back again
and turned to an article about old buildings. "Aha!" he
grinned. "This article isn't about people."

"I'll bet you see people in it before you turn the page."

Al read silently. The smile on his face faded when he
reached the sixth paragraph which mentioned politicians, real
estate owners, contractors and manufacturers. Subsequent
paragraphs talked about preservationists, historians, architects
and city planners. He put the magazine down. "You're right,"

he said.

"Let's talk about the close," Dave continued. "I like to end a paper on a high note. That's the last chance you have to make a positive impression. People tend to remember what they read last, so I try to save my best, most powerful illustration for the conclusion."

"I've always had a hard time with endings," said Joanne.

"I agree; they're hard. Often I wait to write the conclusion until after the first draft, when I'm rewriting and polishing the paper. You might look for a quote that summarizes your thesis. Or you could draw a conclusion from the facts you've presented. However, don't say any more than necessary. I always think it's best to stop when you've made your point. So don't ramble."

"I think I'm going to be sick," said Al, shaking his head. "I was with you until this week. But I'll never be good at papers."

"Don't say that!" said Joanne with a forcefulness that surprised the two men. "You express yourself well when you talk. I mean, you're funny, but you also think well and the things you have to say are important. You've put the other principles into practice. You can do it with papers, too. It just takes some practice."

"Well, maybe. . ."

"Not maybe. You *can* do it."

Dave laughed at Al's shocked expression. "She's right. Give it a try and let us know how it goes. For your next paper, when you have a little more time, I can give you a couple more techniques. And maybe Joanne can tell us some of the things she does when she writes her papers."

7

SOLVING PROBLEMS AND MAKING DECISIONS

"Well, Mentor, I finished my paper," Al said as he met Dave at the entrance to the student union building. Joanne had not arrived, so they stood and talked for a moment in the crisp fall air.

"How did it go?" asked Dave.

"Your suggestions helped me get organized. I haven't gotten the paper back yet, but I think I did all right."

They saw Joanne running towards them. "Sorry I'm late," she said. "I'm having problems with my car."

"What's wrong?" asked Dave.

"I don't know. It's so old and worn out. It started okay this morning and I drove it down here because I had to run an errand before our meeting. But when I tried to start it a few minutes ago, nothing happened. Sometimes I wonder how much longer it will last."

"Mind if I take a look?" Al asked.

"Would you mind? I'd really appreciate it. I need to be able to get to work."

The three walked over to the parking lot. Al asked for the keys and tried to start the car. The starter motor fluttered but the engine wouldn't turn over. "Well, we know the ignition switch works," said Al.

"How do you know that?" asked Joanne.

"If it wasn't working, nothing would have happened. It sounds to me like your battery is weak. Did you leave your lights on?"

"No."

"Have you had trouble starting the car lately?"

"The last few days it's been starting a little slow."

"Have you got jumper cables in your car, Dave?"

"Yes. I'll get them."

Al turned to Joanne and said, "Let's get your car started first. Then we'll see if we can locate the problem."

It took only a minute for Dave to drive his car over. As Al attached the cables, he noted that the posts on Joanne's car battery were clean. "You don't have any corrosion. If you did, that would wear the battery down." He reached down and tugged on the fan belt. "Fan belt appears to be okay, so your problem is either the alternator or a dead battery."

Al slipped into the driver's seat and started the car. He examined the gauge on the dash as he revved the engine for a moment. "I think the alternator is feeding juice to the battery. But the battery isn't holding the charge." He got out of the car and shut the hood. "How long have you had this battery?" he asked.

"It was in the car when I bought it three years ago."

"I'm not 100 percent sure, but it looks like you'll probably need a new battery. They can hook it up to a tester at the shop and tell you. The only other possibility is a short that might be draining the battery. After our meeting, we'll start your car again and Dave can follow you over to the shop."

As the three of them walked back to the student union, Dave asked Joanne and Al to analyze what had just taken place. "Al, you used a basic principle with Joanne's car, and you can use that principle in any situation where you need to solve a problem."

"I don't understand," said Joanne.

"Start at the beginning and tell me how Al discovered what was wrong with your car."

"Well, first he tried to start it. When he heard a noise in the starter, he knew it wasn't the ignition."

"That's right. So Al eliminated one possible cause. What did he do next?"

"He asked me some questions. He wanted to know if I'd

left my lights on, and if I'd had difficulty starting the car lately."

"And what did he learn by doing that?"

"He eliminated the possibility that I might have drained the battery by leaving my lights on."

"Good. Then what?"

"He started checking other possibilities," she continued. "He examined the battery terminals for corrosion. Then he checked the fan belt and it was all right. So he figured that the problem was either with the alternator or because of a dead battery, or possibly a short. He started the car and checked the battery gauge and suggested I have the battery tested to see if it should be replaced."

"What was Al looking for through this process?"

"The cause of my problem."

"That's correct. Notice that Al assumed each symptom had a cause and he continued checking until he couldn't go any further. The reason is that, when you correct the cause, you eliminate the symptoms."

All three bought soft drinks, then found a table in the corner of the coffee shop. Dave pulled out a sheet of paper from his briefcase. "In light of what we're discussing, I think you'll enjoy something a friend gave me. It's a series of actual statements from auto insurance accident forms.* The people involved were asked to describe in a few words what caused their accidents. Here is what some of them said:

" 'Coming home, I drove into the wrong house, and collided with a tree I don't have.'

" 'The guy was all over the road: I had to swerve a number of times before I hit him.'

" 'I had been driving my car for four years when I fell asleep at the wheel and had an accident.' "

Al started laughing at that one, and Jo was smiling. Dave continued.

" 'The pedestrian had no idea what direction to go, so I ran over him.'

" 'The telephone pole was approaching fast. I was attempt-

*From *Toronto Sunday*, July 26, 1977.

ing to swerve out of its path when it struck my front end.'

" 'I was on my way to the doctor's with rear end trouble when my universal joint gave way, causing me to have an accident.' "

Al, his arms folded over his stomach, was doubled up in laughter. Joanne and Dave couldn't help laughing at Al's reaction.

Finally they calmed down. Dave made the point that problem-solving is often difficult because people can't seem to find causes easily. "A good friend of mine had a heart attack recently. He's only forty-eight years old, so you can imagine how this scared him. He wanted to understand what caused the heart attack, so he had a long talk with his doctor. What do you think the doctor told him?"

Joanne suggested that the problem was too much cholesterol, which caused the blood vessels to clog. "The solution could be to cut back on foods such as butter and eggs and cheese," she said.

"Actually, the doctor did prescribe a diet, but cholesterol wasn't the cause of my friend's heart attack. The doctor said there was a much more significant factor — stress. Apparently stress affects the body's chemical balance in such a way that a higher cholesterol level occurs in the blood stream. The doctor told my friend that he would have to reduce his exposure to high pressure situations and learn to relax. He's what you would call a workaholic. He didn't know how to keep balance in his life."

Dave suggested that Al and Joanne write this principle on a card:

```
┌─────────────────────────────────────────┐
│                                         │
│              SEEK CAUSES                │
│                                         │
│        Consider every problem a         │
│          symptom.                       │
│        Search for a cause for every     │
│          symptom.                       │
│                                         │
└─────────────────────────────────────────┘
```

"Once you've isolated the cause, you're ready to solve the problem," Dave observed. "Joanne, if you didn't know the cause of your car problem, you might keep jump-starting the car. Or you might assume there's something wrong with the alternator. Or you might try to recharge the battery and it would keep losing its charge. You would not solve your problem.

"This is a principle I use all the time in business. When someone says, 'I have a problem,' I have discovered that it is almost always a symptom rather than the real problem. So I treat it as a symptom, and I look for what causes that symptom. Once I find the cause I am tempted to think that now I have found the real problem, but I have learned that that 'cause' is often a symptom, too, so I look for what causes *that* symptom. I keep going like this until I cannot find a deeper cause and then I can assume I have isolated the real problem. You can use this process in school to solve problems, write papers, and answer exam questions."

Joanne said she had a homework problem in economics and wondered if this process might help. "The case concerns Germany after World War I. Within four years, the wholesale price index rose from one mark to more than one trillion marks. The question we have to answer is 'What caused the hyperinflation?' We also have to evaluate which of two theories provides a more helpful analysis of the problem."

Dave answered, "You certainly can use the process we've discussed. First of all, you would need to define what you mean by inflation. I assume your professor has done that for you. Then take each of the symptoms and see if you can determine the cause. Systematically work your way back until you can't go any further."

"I'll give it a try," Joanne said.

"Dave, I wonder if you could help me solve a personal problem." Al pulled out a sheet of paper. "I'm preregistering for next term. I have to choose one more class and I have three options. I can't decide which one to select."

"Well, Al, we've talked about seeking causes, but that only applies when there's a problem. There really isn't a *problem* here; there is a *decision* to make. You want to choose which course to take. Whenever I have to make a decision, I use a different technique. I suggest you write it on a card, then I'll explain how it works.

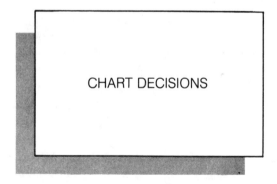

CHART DECISIONS

"Let's talk about your situation. What are your choices?"

"One is Humanities 101; it's required for my degree. The other two classes are in my major. Engineering 203 is required. Engineering 235 is optional, but I'm really interested in the subject, and it's offered only every other year."

"Joanne, what do you think he should do?"

"I took that humanities class last year. It was a fantastic course. You'll love it!"

"Thanks a lot!" Al said in a tone that revealed his lack of enthusiasm.

"You obviously aren't too excited about that class, are you Al?" asked Dave. "You're only considering it because it's required. It would be very tempting to make your decision according to your surface desires rather than by using some clearly defined objectives."

"You mean I shouldn't consider what I want to do in the decision?"

"No, that's not what I mean. Your desires should be part of your objectives. But let's take look at it. To do that, we need to chart it."

Dave took a yellow pad from his briefcase and drew the following chart:

		Alternatives		
		Hum. 101	Eng. 203	Eng. 235
Objectives	Required			
	Unavailability			
	Major			
	Interest			

"Here's what I think I hear you saying. You have three alternatives. Humanities 101 is an overall school requirement. Engineering 203 is required for your major. Engineering 235 is in your major field, but not required. Now let's list your objectives in the left column. Apparently one objective is to complete a requirement for graduation. A second is the availability or unavailability of the course in the next two years. Third is how it contributes to your major. And fourth is your interest in the subject. Did I get them all?"

"That's about it. . . . Oh, there is one other thing. Next term is basketball season. I'm concerned that I don't get a work load that's more than I can handle."

"Then we'd better write down 'work load' as one of the criteria. Can you think of anything else?"

Al was silent for a moment. "No, I think that about covers it."

"Then let's see how this charts out. The first two courses are required for graduation, the third is not. Right?"

Al nodded, so Dave wrote a " + " on the first line under Humanities 101 and under Engineering 203, and a "-" under Engineering 235.

"Let me explain what I'm doing. The plus sign means that this particular alternative satisfies the objective. The minus sign means it doesn't. Now what about availability or unavailability?"

"Well, the humanities course is offered every term."

"So we'll put down a minus, because you can take it any time. In other words, based only on that objective, you would not tend to choose that particular alternative."

"Engineering 235 won't be offered again until my senior year."

"So that's a plus for the decision, because you might want more flexibility your senior year. What about Engineering 203?"

"It's offered once a year. I could take it now, or next year. It's a basic course, so I shouldn't wait until my senior year."

"Is there a strong positive or negative there?" Dave asked.

"Neither, really."

"Let me introduce another symbol to you. It's a zero. We

use it when there isn't a clear-cut plus or minus. So here's
where we are so far:

		Alternatives		
		Hum. 101	Eng. 203	Eng. 235
Objectives	Required	+	+	-
	Unavailability	–	0	+
	Major			
	Interest			
	Work Load			

"Let's keep going," Dave encouraged. "Does the class
contribute to your major? That's a minus for humanities,
pluses for the other two. Right?"

"Right."

"How about interest?"

"Well, definitely minus on humanities."

Joanne cleared her throat.

"I don't feel one way or the other about the middle choice,"
Al continued. "And I'm definitely interested in the third one."

"Minus. Zero. Plus. And work load?"

"Joanne, how much work is this humanities course?"

"It's not hard at all. Some reading. Just two tests, a couple
of papers."

"That's a plus," Al admitted. "Both of the other courses
require labs. I know they both would mean more work."

"Okay, let's see what we've got." Dave said.

		Alternatives		
		Hum. 101	Eng. 203	Eng. 235
	Required	+	+	-
Objectives	Unavailability	-	0	+
	Major	-	+	+
	Interest	-	0	+
	Work Load	+	-	-
	TOTAL	-1	+1	+1

"Looks like number one is out, but we've got a tie between the other two," said Al.

"So you don't have a decision, yet. Let's think about the objectives. Are they all equal in importance?"

"Oh no!" Al leaned back and slapped his forehead. "The 80/20 Rule. How could I forget!"

Dave laughed at the act. "You're learning! It might help to prioritize your objectives. If one or two of the objectives are more important, you might want to double their value; perhaps give two plusses or two minuses. But rather than doing that now, why don't we make that your assignment for next week? Make another decision chart and when we get back together, let us know what you decide.

"And Joanne, you have your 'Seek Causes' assignment on your economics problem."

"Yes, and I can see where this decision chart will be valuable to me also. I often spend hours and hours debating a particular decision. Now I can picture taking only minutes and being more sure I make the right choice."

Dave smiled as he drove home. The techniques he was teaching Al and Joanne were part of the reason for his success in business. If they used them well in class, these two young people would increase their comprehension and certainly wouldn't hurt their grades. But knowing how to seek causes and chart decisions would remain valuable to them long after graduation. Those tools would prove useful in every area of life.

8

BEING CREATIVE

"How's your car running?" Al asked Joanne as they entered the student union.

"You were right; I had to have the battery replaced. The car runs great now. And did you make your decision?"

Al pulled out a sheet of paper and showed it to Joanne and Dave.

		Alternatives		
		Hum. 101	Eng. 203	Eng. 235
Objectives	Required (2x)	++	++	--
	Major	–	+	+
	Unavailability	–	0	+
	Interest	–	0	+
	TOTAL	-1	+3	+1

"You decided on the basic engineering course," observed Dave.

"Yes. Here's what I did. First I prioritized my objectives. I realized that I wanted to make significant progress toward my degree, and that meant that taking a required course was more important. So I doubled its value. That's what the '2X' symbol stands for. Also, I eliminated one objective. Since I'm learning how to work smarter, not harder, I felt that work load wasn't an important factor in this decision. So it's Engineering 203, and I feel good about that choice. I need to lay a strong foundation in my major so I'm prepared for some of the optional courses later on.

"And how did you do on your econ assignment, Joanne?"

"You won't believe it! I got my first *A* in the class. The principle we learned last week kept me looking beyond the symptoms of inflation to the cause, or in this case, causes. Dr. Bolger said he liked my systematic way of thinking."

"Congratulations," Al offered. "By the way, I got my paper back."

"And...?"

"I'm improving; I got a *B*. Here's what the instructor wrote at the top: 'Best paper you've done. But I'd like to see some more creativity.' I'm afraid I'm not that creative. And I've got another paper due in ten days."

Dave had a suggestion. "Joanne, you seem to be quite creative. Can you help?"

Joanne asked Al to explain the subject of his last paper.

"Napoleon. I wrote about his military skill."

"What approach did you take?"

Al spread out his hands in resignation. "Just gave some facts. Used some good quotes. I tried to make it exciting, Dave, like you said. But you've got to get your footnotes in and everything. It was just your basic paper."

"Did you ever consider taking an interview approach?" Joanne asked. "Pose questions and have Napoleon answer them, using your historical sources. You'd still have your footnotes, but it would make more interesting reading. I used that technique last year when I wrote a paper about Ernest Hemingway. I 'interviewed' him about his writing style and pulled his answers from various things he'd written."

"Wow! How do you think up such ideas?"

"I don't know. They just seem to come."

"That's typical for a creative person," said Dave. "However, you can learn to be more creative, Al. Let's do some cards on creativity. Here's the first one:

CULTIVATE CREATIVE
THINKING

"Joanne, something triggered that idea, to do the interview format. Try to think of what it was."

Joanne thought for a moment before answering. "I saw that same technique used once in a magazine article about Jack London. It was three or four years ago, but that's probably where my idea came from."

"So you pick up ideas from your reading?"

"I guess I do. Earlier this year, I used a narrative approach in one paper I did. I had all the facts, but I thought it was more interesting to weave them into a story, like you often see in a historical novel."

"Al, what Joanne is demonstrating is that she has prepared her mind to be creative. In farming, what does it mean when we say a farmer cultivates his soil?"

"He breaks up the dirt between the rows in the field and destroys the weeds so that his crops can grow better," Al answered.

"That's right. It's the same idea with creative thinking. We tend to become locked in to certain ways of seeing and doing things. If you want to be creative, you need to 'break up the soil' so to speak. Joanne just demonstrated one way. Reading will give you ideas to stimulate your thinking. I have a friend who is a professional writer. He often writes articles about celebrities. When he wants a fresh approach, he reads personality profiles in several magazines and usually finds several ideas for the article he's writing.

"I know you're not an avid reader," Dave continued, "but you could pick up a book on creativity. Several years ago, I was teaching a class and I decided I wanted to improve as a teacher. I bought two books on teaching techniques, and nearly every week I looked through them for ideas. I tried all kinds of things. One time we did a skit. Another time we took a survey. I used a case study. Agree-disagree questions. I'm not naturally that creative so I wouldn't have thought of those ideas without help."

"I thought you had to think up your own ideas to be creative," Al said.

"Actually, there aren't a lot of truly original ideas. What your history professor wants is a fresh approach. He realizes that, if you will break out of your set pattern, you'll probably gain some new insights. Thomas Edison once said that genius is 2 percent inspiration and 98 percent perspiration. So don't think that creativity is something you can't develop. It improves with practice. You can start by cultivating your thoughts, by getting outside input to force your mind to think in new ways.

"One thing I do to stimulate my thinking in business is to brainstorm with associates. You could do that with a couple of other students. In fact, why don't we try that right now? Al, what's the topic for your next paper?"

"It's about peasant life in eighteenth-century England. How can I possibly be creative on that subject?"

Joanne immediately had an idea. "Why not describe one day in the life of a peasant?"

"Great idea!" said Dave. "Another approach might be to do a comparison. Contrast the peasants and the ruling class.

You might cover areas like food, clothing, income, shelter, and so on."

"Or how about using a personal illustration?" said Joanne.

"What do you mean?" asked Al. "I wasn't alive back then."

"You could compare a peasant's life with your own," she suggested. "Try thinking of some experiences you have had that might help you understand how people lived and felt two hundred years ago. After all, they were people just like us. There must be some similarities. In turn, that might help you understand the differences better. Think of some common activities. Fishing. Farming. Ask questions like 'How did they keep warm? How did they cook?' Compare them to your experiences."

"Look what happened," Dave observed. "We just came up with three ideas for your next paper. You may not use any of them, but they might stimulate you to think of some other ideas. Now here's one more thing I do. I always carry several three-by-five cards with me."

"I hadn't noticed!" quipped Al.

Dave pulled a couple of cards from his coat jacket. "Here's one with ideas I've jotted down for my next paper. Another has ideas for a class I'm teaching. Whenever I see or hear something I think might be useful for those two areas, I jot it down. Sometimes in my office I'll take a stack of cards, write one idea about a subject or a particular problem on each card, then lay them out on a large table. I'll experiment with various combinations to see if I see any new patterns or relationships."

"I don't know," Al said. "This will take some practice."

"That's true," said Dave. "But let me suggest some more ways you can stimulate creativity. Here's our second card:

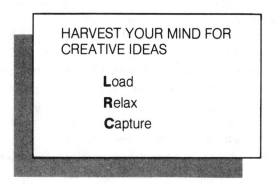

HARVEST YOUR MIND FOR
CREATIVE IDEAS

Load
Relax
Capture

"Have you ever heard of R. G. LeTourneau?"

Joanne hadn't, but Al recalled that he was an inventor of earth-moving equipment. "Wasn't he famous for his creative thinking?" he asked.

"Yes, he was. Let me give you an example of how his mind worked. A friend of LeTourneau's was traveling by plane with him one night. LeTourneau took a nap on the flight, and after about half an hour, he took a notebook from his pocket, made some notes, then returned the notebook to his pocket. But his friend noticed that LeTourneau did not look at the notebook while he wrote; he seemed to be staring into space. This scene was repeated three more times before they landed.

"When LeTourneau awoke, his friend mentioned the incident. The inventor seemed surprised, but he pulled out the notebook from his pocket. When he saw what he'd written, he exclaimed, 'There it is! I have been waiting for this information for more than a month.'

"What LeTourneau did was harvest his mind for creative ideas. You can do the same thing by loading information about a subject into your mind. The most common way to do that is by reading all you can about a subject. Then you relax. Don't think about it for a while. You might take a nap or play some basketball or listen to some music. After a period of time, ideas will start to come. Sometimes it takes only a few minutes before this happens; usually, however, it's a little longer.

"When you get the ideas," Dave summarized, "capture them by writing them down. Often you'll find that ideas come when you're doing something else and it's not necessarily convenient to stop. But if you don't write them down, you'll probably lose them. All three — load, relax and capture — are necessary to harvest your mind."

"Let me see if I understand," said Al. "Take this paper I'm writing. I'm going to the library tomorrow to get some material. I'll make some notes on index cards and probably check out a couple of books. You're saying I should load all of that into my mind and then don't worry about it for . . .for how long?"

"That depends," said Dave. "Sometimes it's just an hour or two. Other times one or two days. Often I load my mind in the evening, right before I go to sleep. I keep a note pad by my bed in case I get any ideas at night. In fact, my wife gave me a pen with a light at the end so I can see what I write. But once I've loaded, I relax in some way. Sometimes when I'm relaxing with the newspaper or talking with my wife, I'll suddenly get some ideas on something I've thought about earlier."

"I guess what worries me is the last part," Al confessed. "What if I don't get any bright ideas?"

"You'd better write this down," suggested Dave.

PUSH MENTAL BOUNDARIES

"What does that mean?"

"Let me give an example. Do you remember that big hailstorm we had the second week of school?"

"I've got a number of dents in my car from it," said Joanne.

"I was parked over by the administration building," Dave recalled. "When the hail started, I ran out and moved the car underneath a large tree. Unfortunately, as you remember, those hailstones were so big that the tree didn't give me enough protection. My car also received some dents. Afterward, as I was moving the car back to my regular parking spot, I noticed the pedestrian walkway that runs right underneath the administration building. It would have provided perfect protection for my car, but I didn't think of it. Why? Because sidewalks are for people . . . except in hailstorms. There was a curbing there that prevented me from seeing that possibility on that occasion. It makes me wonder how many curbings or boundaries we put on our minds.

"Creativity, by definition, is pushing beyond traditional boundaries. One of the best ways to be creative is to assault one of the boundaries directly. Otherwise, that boundary keeps us from going any further in a given direction; it forms a curbing in our mind."

"So how do you go about doing that?" Joanne asked.

"One way to push mental boundaries is to play the 'What if?' game," Dave noted. "Sometimes when we're trying to solve a problem in my business, I'll ask, 'What if resources were not a problem? How could we solve this?' When we don't have to worry about money or manpower — the usual boundaries or curbings that stand in our way — we often think of new ideas, and sometimes we're surprised at how economical they turn out to be.

"Another idea is the 'Why not?' approach. A basic ground rule when you're brainstorming is that you don't criticize any idea. Sometimes I take it one step further. With any idea, I say, 'Why not?' Just because it hasn't been done, or it's different, doesn't mean it's a bad idea. Take your paper, Al. When Joanne suggested using a personal illustration, you could have said, 'That's not the way I write papers.' But you seemed open to that idea. You in effect said, 'Why not?' By considering an unorthodox option, you stretched your mental boundaries."

"We've covered a lot of new ground today," said Al.

"Here's one way you can remember what we've discussed," Dave responded. "Picture a farmer with a tractor planting his field. The sowing of seeds, that's loading. Then you relax — there's not a whole lot you can do to make the seeds grow. When the ideas are ready, capture them, just like a farmer harvests his crops. And you might remember the final principle — push mental boundaries — by imagining that farmer storing his harvest in a barn and there being such an abundant crop that it is bursting through the sides of the barn. So the farmer tries to push back the walls — the boundaries — so there's room to store it all."

"That's kind of wild!" said Al. "But I like it!"

"And let me add this. When you work at being creative like this, you will have more fun in school!"

Al laughed. "I just thought of something. I wonder what kind of sports they had in eighteenth-century England? They must have done something for recreation. I wonder if the kids played sports. I know how I feel when I play basketball; that might be a way to help me relate to those peasants."

"Great idea!" said Joanne. "Now you're cooking! Play around with that idea and see what happens."

"I have a suggestion," said Dave. "Rather than my meeting with you next week, why don't you two get together on your own. Al, do as much work as you can on your paper, then get together with Joanne and discuss it."

"You're not going to believe this," said Al. "I'm actually itching to get started. I'll try to have the paper written next week so we can go over it. And I may even have the grade when we meet again in two weeks."

9

LIKING
WHAT YOU DO

Al waved his history paper in the air as he, Joanne and Dave converged at the student union entrance. "You won't believe it!" he shouted. "I just got the paper back this morning. I got an *A!*. Dr. Sears said he loved it!"

"This calls for a celebration!" said Dave. "Let's walk over to Jack's Ice Cream Shop. I'll treat."

As the three entered the quaint business district just off campus, Dave inquired about Al and Jo's meeting the previous week. "It sounds like it was beneficial."

"I decided to write about a day in the life of an English peasant," said Al. "I had all the facts researched, but Joanne helped me put some feeling into it.

"By the way, I wrote the paper in the morning. I read through all my notes the night before. Then as I went to sleep, I imagined myself living two hundred years ago in England. When I woke up, I could hardly wait to start writing. It was so much easier than I thought it would be."

"Did you do anything with your sports idea?"

"Yes, I did some research on the subject and made that a part of the day."

"Joanne, did you learn anything through this experience?" Dave asked.

"Yes, I've gained some real insight into the creative process. For instance, you told us to cultivate creative thinking. I'd never thought about why I was more creative at certain times. One thing I realized last week was that I need a creative setting in which to work. I've decorated my room with some posters, but when the room is messy, I don't write very well. There's also a little cafe near campus where I can go when I'm not feeling very creative. A couple of hours there usually cures the problem. So I guess the setting is important to help me be more creative."

"Do you see the benefit you two gained by working together?" Dave continued. "That's why I suggested you meet without me. I wanted you to see how you can improve your weaknesses and use your strengths. Al, you recognized a weakness in creative writing and you were able to compensate for that weakness by learning from Joanne. Learning from someone else is something you can always do. And it's one of the principles for you to remember.

> FIND HELP FOR YOUR
> WEAKNESSES

"There are many ways to do that. You can read about an area in which you are weak. Or attend a seminar. Experiment with several techniques to see which ones help you most. One excellent method is to be tutored, but you often can gain the same benefit by studying with a student who's strong in your area of weakness. That's what you did with Joanne, Al.

"Joanne, you were intuitively doing some things right, but by teaching Al, you learned a lot about your strength. There's a powerful principle here. When you teach, you not only help that person, but you benefit because you gain further understanding. In fact, that's a principle of life. When you give, you end up receiving in return."

At Jack's, Joanne had a single-scoop cone, Dave a small sundae, and Al ordered a deluxe banana split. As Dave finished his ice cream, Al was still savoring the chocolate portion of his banana split. "You really like ice cream, don't you, Al?" said Dave.

"I love it!"

"Do you ever get tired of eating ice cream?"

"Never. I wouldn't mind eating it every day."

"If ice cream had all the basic nutrients you needed, do you think you could live on it?"

"You bet. What a way to go!"

"Have you noticed that some of your activities are like that? You really enjoy doing them."

"Like playing basketball, especially a good pick-up game."

"Have you also noticed that some things you simply don't like to do? You might call them 'liver activities.' They kind of sit on the plate and quiver."

"Yuck!" said Joanne. She was glad she'd finished her cone.

"Would you be interested in taking those liver chores and turning them into ice cream activities?" Dave continued.

Al was now scooping out the last syrupy spoonfuls from the bottom of his dish. "I'm all ears, Mentor. What do you have in mind?"

"One thing I promised you was that you'd have more fun. We've realized that by employing the 80/20 Rule we are giving priority to the activities that promise the highest benefit, and often that frees us to do other things we enjoy. But sometimes there's no getting around an activity we don't particularly enjoy. Wouldn't it be great if we could learn to like those things, too?"

"Like losing ten pounds?" said Joanne. That's why she'd had only one scoop of ice cream, and she felt a little guilty about that.

"Or running wind sprints at the end of basketball practice," said Al.

"Those are good examples. The key to doing anything we don't like is that we need to be motivated. And the best motivation is internal rather than external. Let's talk about how we can be motivated internally in those two activities. Can you think of any?"

"Sometimes the coach yells at us," said Al. "It motivates me because I want to make the team. However, if he promised me a banana split after practice, I might push even harder in those sprints."

"That's no help at all," said Joanne. "No one's pushing me, and food is my problem, especially late-night snacks after I'm done studying."

"We talked a few weeks ago about giving yourself a reward after you reach a goal," Dave said. "Sometimes that helps. But I'm thinking of something more basic than that. We need to keep before us *why* we're doing what we're doing. Let me give an example that Joanne might relate to. A couple of years ago, my wife and I took a trip to Hawaii. Mary was conscious of her appearance and wanted to lose some weight before we left. In order to stay motivated, she cut out of a magazine a picture of a woman sunning herself on Waikiki Beach, and she attached that picture to the refrigerator door. It was a constant reminder of her goal and helped her lose the weight."

"She was constantly aware of the benefit of not overeating and eating the right kinds of foods," Joanne remarked.

"That's exactly right. And that's the first way to motivate yourself to do something you don't like. Remember why you're doing it. If you don't remember why something is important, it's much harder to do it. Al, what's the purpose of those wind sprints?"

"I think everyone on the team would like to know that. Probably to help with our conditioning. But just knowing it's good for you doesn't make it any easier to run when you're tired."

"Can you think of any other benefits from those sprints?"

Al thought for a moment. "The coach sometimes reminds

us of how tired we can be near the end of the game. Yet that's when we need to give an extra effort if we want to win."

"Perhaps it might help to think of that when the coach tells you to line up for sprints at the end of practice. You might visualize yourself in the last two minutes of an important game when you need to give it all you've got, even though you're exhausted. Joanne, what's the benefit for you?"

"I actually feel better when I weigh less, and I feel better about myself."

"So remembering why you're doing what you're doing helps you to be motivated naturally. But sometimes it takes more than that. Often it helps to enlist a friend. When possible, do the things you don't like with someone you do like. Al, do you have a good friend on the team?"

"Yeah, Bob and I are pretty close."

"You might line up next to each other and do those sprints together. I do that almost every day when I jog. I have a running partner who is at the same speed and distance level that I am. We enjoy talking as we run. Our friendship keeps us coming out every morning rather than sleeping an extra hour.

"Jo, you could do the same thing with your diet. You probably have at least one girl friend who also is struggling with her weight. You might help each other by eating a salad together at lunch. It's a little harder to give in to temptation when a friend is right there with you.

"Now, here's one more idea. Make a game out of what you have to do. Al, you and Bob might see who can win the most sprints in a given week."

"No, that wouldn't work," Al said. "Bob's faster. I'd be glad to beat him just once a week."

"Then make that your goal. Try to beat him once this week. If you do that, try for two."

"How do you make a game out of dieting?" asked Joanne.

"Al, do you have any suggestions?"

"She could have a contest with her friend to see who loses the most weight in a week."

"I don't like that kind of competition," said Joanne. "I don't think I could do it."

"I appreciate that," said Dave. "I should clarify that a game doesn't mean you're competing against someone. It might be a game you play with yourself, for your own motivation. For instance, I don't enjoy making phone calls, but in my job I have to make a lot of calls every day. What's discouraging is that I never see the end of those calls, which is hard for someone like me who's goal-oriented. I might return twenty calls in an afternoon, and many of those will require me to make further calls. And on top of that, more calls will have come in while I'm making the first batch of calls. I feel no sense of progress.

"So, here's what I did. I started keeping a tally sheet by my phone. Every time I dialed a number, I put a mark on that sheet. It didn't matter if I got a busy signal or a wrong number. Even if I dialed information, I got a mark. My game was to see how many marks I could record in a day. My personal record is 64. On a busy day when I go over 50, I start wondering if I can break my record. That may sound corny, but it does make phone calls more enjoyable for me because I have tangible evidence of how many calls I've made, regardless of how many are left."

"I could do that by setting a personal weight-loss goal for the week," said Joanne. "Something realistic, like losing three pounds. And instead of weighing myself every morning, I could have a weigh-in day every week and keep a little chart of my progress."

"You've got the right idea," said Dave.

"I wonder if I could apply this to my job at Burger Boy," Joanne continued. "Sometimes I think if I have to cook another hamburger, I'll scream. I turn hamburgers in my sleep."

"Let's see if we can apply all three motivations to this job. First, what benefits do you get from your work?"

"I couldn't go to school without it. I need the money."

Dave gave Joanne an index card and suggested she write that reason down. "Can you think of any other benefits?"

"Not really."

"Does your job benefit anyone besides you?"

"I suppose those who are hungry."

"Is providing a service to people who are in a hurry and need something to eat a benefit?"

"I guess. I hadn't thought about it."

"Do any of your friends come into the restaurant to eat?"

"Sometimes. We're near campus, so there are some commuters who stop in almost every day."

"Do you have a student loan?" asked Dave.

"No. I didn't want to owe any money when I finished school."

"So there's another benefit. By working now, you'll be debt-free when you graduate. That will relieve you of a lot of pressure."

"I'm getting the picture. You want me to write all of these things down on the card?"

"Yes, and then I suggest you put that card someplace where you will see it often. Maybe on the mirror in your room. Or on the dashboard of your car."

"How does the second part fit, doing it with someone you like?" she asked.

"You may not have control over that. There may be some activities you have to do yourself, like when I make phone calls. However, you do enjoy people, don't you? Why don't you see if you can learn something interesting about your customers."

"With some people that's easier than with others."

"You may not succeed with all of them, but see how many will respond to your smile and a cheerful greeting. Besides, your employer will love it."

"I have an idea," said Al. "What's the biggest order you had yesterday? Did anyone buy more than 10 hamburgers?"

"I don't remember."

"Why don't you keep track today."

"I don't get it. Why would I want to do that?"

"Al's idea is to make a game of it," said Dave. "Do you know how much money is spent in fast-food restaurants these days? It's unbelievable. Nearly 100 billion dollars each year. Maybe you can learn a little about that by keeping track of how many hamburgers your customers buy. See how many buy one. How many buy two. And so on."

"Dave, we've forgotten to write the principles out on a three-by-five card," Al said as he wrote the following:

LEARN TO LIKE WHAT YOU DO

Remember why

Enlist a friend

Make a game of it

"I thought of a way to remember this," Al said. "Do you see the acrostic?"

"REM? That doesn't mean anything to me," said Joanne.

Dave couldn't recall the exact definition but remembered that it had something to do with radiation.

"It stands for 'Roentgen Equivalent, Man,' " declared Al. "It's a dose of radiation which produces a biological effect."

Joanne laughed. "You do know your science! I may not understand what a rem is, but I think it will help me remember today's lesson. I must admit this has been an unusual session. I've never really thought about making the things I don't like to do more enjoyable."

"I don't have to teach you how to be motivated to do the things you enjoy doing," said Dave. "Just like I don't have to tell Al to eat all of his ice cream. He does that naturally because he likes it. But very few people tell us how to be motivated to do what we don't like to do. We're advised to tough it out, or be disciplined. Or there's the general concept of doing it because 'it's good for you.' Yet I think this concept is a good way to have more fun — in college, or anywhere."

"Do you have an assignment for us?" asked Al.

"Try the technique this week. Al, see how it goes with your wind sprints, and also use these three principles on some other activity. Joanne, I'd like to see how you do with your job. If you're spending many hours a week at one task, it would be well worth it to try making it more enjoyable."

10

COPING WITH ANXIETY

Al munched on a sandwich while he and Dave waited for Joanne to arrive. "I had to skip lunch to run an errand," said Al. "I'm starved."

"How's basketball going?" asked Dave.

"Practice is going well and I'm holding my own in the scrimmages. There's no guarantee I'll make the final cut, but I like my chances. By the way, I beat Bob on the final sprint yesterday. I told him I was going to catch him but he couldn't believe I actually did it. I think the competition helps us both. What are we going to cover today?"

"Well, finals are coming up soon."

"And I can sure use some help getting ready. It's tension time, especially in my math class where the final is 50 percent of our grade."

"I thought I'd teach you how to peak on tests."

"You mean sit next to someone smart and look over his shoulder?"

"That's peek with two *E*'s," Dave laughed. "I'm talking about peak, spelled *P-E-A-K*."

"I don't understand why Jo is late. She's usually so punctual. Even the day her car wouldn't start, she was only a couple of minutes late."

Dave saw Joanne enter the coffee shop. She spotted the two men at the corner table, came over and sat down, but said nothing. Her eyes were red from crying.

"Hi, Joanne. Is everything okay?" said Dave.

"No, everything is *not* okay. Jim broke up with me. He's dating my best friend."

99

"Hey, he's no big loss," joked Al. "There must be a dozen other guys lining up to take you out."

"Oh, shut up!" Joanne was trying hard to keep from crying again.

"Did this just happen?" asked Dave.

"Two days ago. I've been a mess since. I can't seem to pull myself together. Jim and I have econ together right before I come over here. He just ignored me, pretended I never even existed."

"That has to hurt." Al noticed Dave's genuine concern and decided not to try any more lighthearted jokes. "How have the studies gone the last couple of days?" Dave asked.

"Miserable. I can't concentrate." She pulled out a tissue and wiped her nose. "I really don't even care right now."

"I can sure understand that. I'll bet you're having trouble sleeping at night."

"How did you know? I'm tired, but every time I try to sleep, my mind goes back to Jim. I want to forget him, but I can't."

"Joanne," Dave spoke gently, "I can't feel exactly what you're feeling right now. But I think I have some idea of what you're going through. Eight months ago my father died. Would you mind if I told you what happened?"

"Go ahead. Maybe it will take my mind off my own problems."

"About two years ago, my father moved out here to live with my family. He had just retired and wanted to be close to the grandchildren. We gave him a room in the back of our house. It was really great to have him around. He was a great handyman, and he did some small remodeling jobs for us. He also improved the landscaping around the yard. Then early this year, he was diagnosed as having cancer. He had a tumor in his back, and it was malignant. The doctors told us it was bad. They would give him radiation treatment twice a week, but there was no guarantee it would help.

"One month to the day after the diagnosis, I got up for my usual morning run. I saw Dad sitting up in bed as I left. I said 'Good morning' and told him I'd be ready to take him to the hospital in about an hour, after I ran and showered. I didn't see him when I returned from my run, so I assumed he was getting ready. I showered and dressed, then went to his room to see if he was ready to go."

Dave stopped for a moment as he felt tears welling up in his eyes. He was surprised at his emotions. The memory of that moment was suddenly very fresh in his mind. "He was dead! I began to panic and I tried to resuscitate him with a heart massage. I remember yelling for Mary, and I was aware of a lot of noise and activity around the house. Then. . . it was like God put his arms around my shoulders and covered my ears. I felt a deep, incredible peace.

"I guess you're never prepared for the loss of someone you really love. But when that moment came for me, God's presence was incredibly real. He gave me the comfort I needed. It was truly amazing."

Al and Joanne were silent. Al had finished his sandwich and was staring into his cup of orange soda and ice. Joanne leaned back in her chair. "I certainly don't have that peace you mentioned," she said. "You say God gave this to you?"

"Yes, God gave it to me. You see, there are some things I can do to deal with worry. Like the pressure of exams coming up in a couple of weeks. But the deeper the anxiety, the more I'm aware that only God can provide deep peace in spite of circumstances."

"It sounds like you have a neat relationship with God. How did it come about?"

"It will take a little while to explain, but I'd love to share it with you."

"If you don't mind, I'm really not into studies today. Maybe this will help me take my mind off Jim."

"You know how much we've talked about being 80/20 Students and determining objectives and listening and reading aggressively and taking good notes. There was a time when I thought that doing those things well was the source of my happiness in life. When I entered State Tech, my goal was to do very well. I was elected vice president of the freshman class. Made the freshman basketball team. Got four *A*s and a *B* the first semester. And I wound up winning the 'Outstanding Freshman' award in the spring.

"When I achieved that goal, I set my sights even higher. There was one trophy that was the most prestigious on campus, and I decided to try and become the second non-senior to win it. I worked hard, using every technique I knew to get the most out of every minute of study. Plus, I was involved in student government, played basketball, was active in my fraternity, and did a fair amount of dating. On top of that, I owned a little concession business in my fraternity. I sold peanuts and candy bars to help pay my way through school. At the end of my junior year, it was announced that I had won the award, and my parents flew out for the ceremony. Have either of you seen the great courtyard at State?"

"I saw it when I checked out the school," said Al. "It's very impressive."

"Then you know how the river runs along one end, and those beautiful ivy-covered buildings make up the other three sides. That's where they have the awards ceremony, right under the dome of the big hall.

"Finally I was called up to receive the award. As I started up the steps to the podium, these words went through my mind with each step I took: 'So what? Big deal! So what?' I thought to myself, 'Good grief! If even in the moment of success it's no big deal, then it's going to be a very empty life.' That got me to wondering, What *is* the source of satisfaction in life?"

Dave paused. Al looked up, troubled. "You mean all these things you're teaching us. . .? I mean, you seem very happy right now."

"Yes, I am happy right now," said Dave, "but let's not confuse success with happiness. I'm teaching you some methods for being successful as students, in terms of learning, making good grades and having more fun. But the true secret to happiness goes far beyond just getting good grades, or playing varsity basketball, or winning a big award. And that relates to the rest of my story."

Leaning back with a smile, Dave relived that momentous summer eleven years ago. "Remember when we first started meeting, I told you about my relationship with God and how it affected my attitude and relationships? Well, it began the summer following my junior year. A girl I was dating spent a lot of time with a group of Christians, so I hung around with them, too. For one thing, they were an attractive group of people. Plus, they played a lot of volleyball, and I like volleyball.

"Several of those college students told me about having a personal relationship with God through Jesus Christ. They talked as if God was giving them guidance every day, giving them peace of mind in tough circumstances, giving them a sense of achievement in life. In fact, Joanne, there was one girl who had just broken up with her boy friend before she came home from college — but she was experiencing deep peace. Frankly, I was impressed. The faith these people had seemed extremely relevant. They were living life in a very full, very desirable way.

"About the middle of the summer — in fact it was the weekend of July fourth — I went to a big party thrown by some friends who lived a few hours drive from my home town. It was in a large, smoke-filled room, and everyone had a drink in their hands. I didn't have a date that night, and one very attractive young lady at the party caught my eye. I noticed she didn't have a date, either, but she was moving from one fellow to another. She'd talk to one for a few minutes, then, obviously disappointed, move on to another. Being an engineer, I projected where she was heading and plotted a course to arrive at the right place at the right time.

"As I started across the room, suddenly it dawned on me. My life was something like hers, moving from one experience to another. I was looking to find satisfaction by achieving different goals, but I wasn't finding it any more than she was.

"Well, to make a long story short, I thought a lot about that incident and about the Christian friends I'd spent time with. I'd tried many things, but I hadn't considered that perhaps God had something to say to me about how I lived my life. I thought about what my Christian friends had told me and I realized that I wasn't satisfied with life because I was doing my own thing. They told me that God had a plan for my life, but I didn't know what that plan was because I was too busy chasing my own goals. They told me that God calls this attitude sin and I needed to accept Christ as God's remedy for that sin.

"Two nights after the party, while lying wide awake in my bed, I prayed: 'God, I need You. I open the door of my life and receive Jesus Christ as my Savior and Lord. Thank You for forgiving my sins. Please take control of my life and make me the person You want me to be. I don't want to continue running from one goal or experience to another, looking for happiness. I want You to give me Your direction and satisfaction as You have given it to my friends. Amen.'

"Well, I didn't exactly float off the bed, but I did get a good night's sleep. And slowly, over the following weeks, my life began to change. For instance, I began to show more love toward my parents and concern for others, not just myself. But I really noticed a change when I returned to school for my senior year."

"Did your grades improve?" said Al. Not quite sure how to react to Dave's story, he couldn't resist a joke even at this serious moment. Joanne, however, was listening intently.

"Actually, Al, it did affect my studies, but in a rather surprising way. There was one class in probability and statistics where we didn't have any feedback on how we were doing for the first six weeks. Imagine fifty highly competitive students in that situation. We were like a bunch of hungry lions when that first exam rolled around.

"I had expected to do well on the test, but I didn't. I

went back to my room very, very frustrated. At that point, I remembered a verse from the Bible that says the result of a person's relationship with God should include love, joy and peace. Well, I certainly wasn't experiencing peace. So I prayed, 'God, I'm not asking for any favors on the exam. But would you please give me Your peace. Amen.' Well, God answered both parts of that prayer. First, He didn't give me any favors on the exam. . . I prayed a lot more intelligently the next time." Al laughed. "Second, He gave me total peace. . . within minutes.

"I guess that was the point when I fully realized that the supernatural God of the universe had come to live within me. He was not some distant being. He was giving me power to cope with my circumstances. I'm sure many others taking that exam were still experiencing the same turmoil I did. But now I had peace.

"That is the same peace God gave me when my father died.

"And God gives me more than just peace. Over the years, I've learned that He is the source of wisdom and understanding. When I don't understand something, I pray to Him and ask for wisdom which He promises to give. That doesn't mean I sit back and do nothing. I work hard to look for answers, solve problems and achieve goals. But while doing that, I realize that I have the privilege of a friendship with the God of all wisdom. So in a very real way, He is the foundation for all I've taught you this term."

Dave stopped talking and let the two sophomores think about his words. Al was the first to speak. "Well, I've never thought much about God. But with exams coming up soon, I might be driven to prayer. I certainly am worried about a couple of my tests."

Joanne looked at her watch and grabbed her books. "I am so sorry, but I've got to go. I really appreciate what you've said. I feel a lot better already."

As she stood, Joanne hesitated for a moment. "Dave, I want to thank you for all your help. You've been so giving. I appreciate all the techniques you've taught us, but I think what's most important is what is at the core of a person's being. You've shown me that core and it explains why you care."

"Thank you, Joanne. I appreciate that." Dave reached into his briefcase and pulled out two small booklets and gave them to Al and Joanne. "I would like you to understand a little more about what I've just shared with you. This booklet tells how you can experience the kind of relationship with God I am experiencing."*

"Thanks," said Joanne as she stood to leave. "I'll read it tonight."

"I will, too," said Al.

"And next week I'll help you get ready for exams."

*See appendix for the text of this booklet.

11

PREPARING
FOR TESTS

"How are you doing, Joanne?" Al didn't wait until they bought their soft drinks and seated themselves in the cafeteria.

"Much better, thanks. I've had a good week. I really appreciate your concern. And thank you, Dave, for your call this week. That meant a lot to me."

When they were settled, Dave brought up the subject that was on everyone's mind. "How is preparation going for exams?"

"Man, am I blitzed," said Al. "I feel like the guy who attended truckdriving school and got surprised on his final exam. Have you ever heard the story?"

"No, I don't think so," Dave said.

"Well, this truck driver's final was an oral exam and here's the question he had to answer: 'You're driving a tractor and rig down a steep mountain road. It's a two-lane road with a steep incline on your left and a sharp drop-off to your right. As you round the curve your brakes fail. At the same moment, you see another fully-loaded truck coming up the hill in its own lane. But it is being passed by another fully-loaded truck coming toward you in your lane. What would you do in that circumstance?'

"The young man thought a moment and then said, 'I'd wake up Leroy!'

" 'Who's Leroy?' asked the instructor.

" 'My partner. He's from a small town and he ain't never seen an accident like this one's gonna be.' "

Joanne and Dave laughed, relieving some of the tension they all were feeling with the approach of finals week. When they stopped laughing, Al said, "I could say you ain't never seen an accident like these finals are going to be for me. Seriously, I am more worried than I'd like to admit."

"I sure understand," said Dave. "My exams are approaching, too. I'd like to share how an 80/20 Student prepares for finals. What do you think is the first thing he does?"

"I have a sneaky suspicion that he doesn't stay up all night cramming," said Al.

"You're partly right. He doesn't stay up all night. However, he does cram, but probably in a different way from what you're used to."

"I've never liked cramming," said Joanne. "If I'm behind, the pressure of trying to catch up and not getting much sleep and worrying whether I've covered everything that's going to be on the test. . . I'm a basket case by the time the exam starts."

"That's right, Joanne. The first thing we must deal with is too much worry, because as you've just demonstrated, worry robs us of energy, focus and motivation. If we can eliminate worries, or at least control them, then we're in a much better position to do well on our tests. There are basically three ways I know to deal with worry. Would you like to write them down?"

"My roommate thinks I'm going to wallpaper our room with these three-by-five cards," joked Al. But he and Joanne carefully took down the three points:

> THREE WAYS TO DEAL WITH WORRY
>
> **D**elete the causes
> **D**isplace the thoughts
> **T**reat the symptoms

"Notice that the first letters of these three techniques spell DDT. That helps me remember them."

"Is that because DDT kills bugs and worry bugs you?" quipped Joanne.

"Hey, I thought I was the one who told the jokes here!" laughed Al. "That's not bad, Jo."

Dave laughed at the exchange. "That's exactly my idea, Joanne. Worry is something like those little gnats that pester us in the summer. I've found these techniques allow me to keep worry under control. The first option is to eliminate, or *Delete the causes* of worry."

"I like that one," said Al with a chuckle. "I'll just eliminate all tests."

"Well, I suppose that is one possible solution," said Dave. "Unfortunately, that's not a very good option if you want to graduate. Another possibility is to eliminate what causes you to be anxious about exams. What are some things that worry you as you prepare for finals?"

"I get uptight when there's a lot of noise in the dorm and I can't concentrate on my work," said Joanne.

"If I wasn't behind in a couple of subjects, that would help," added Al.

"Two good examples. Let's see if we can eliminate these sources of worry. Joanne, what could you do in your situation?"

"I can ask people to quiet down, but they don't always cooperate. When they don't, I have to move to a quiet location, like the library."

"So rather than worrying about the problem, you remove the cause. That's good. What about you, Al?"

"It would help if I'm caught up before the last night, so I can concentrate on review and get some sleep."

"You've got the idea. Let me give you one more example. Once, right before an exam, I had a disagreement with my wife. I found I couldn't concentrate on my studies because I was worried about our problem. I was able to delete this cause by going to Mary, telling her I was sorry and spending a little time resolving the disagreement. I did lose some study time, but I really gained because when I went back to the books, I was able to concentrate totally.

"Now it's not always possible to *Delete the causes* of worry. Like you said, Al, we do have to take tests and there is a certain amount of anxiety associated with them. If you can't delete the cause, then see if you can *Displace the thoughts*. Let's take the following situation. Suppose you wake up at three in the morning and you're worried about an exam. What do you do?"

"I need my rest, so I try to go back to sleep," said Joanne.

"Does that work?"

"Sometimes I toss and turn for an hour or two, and when I do go back to sleep, I usually don't sleep very well."

"One way you could displace that worry would be to get up and study for an hour. Then you would be doing something productive, and I'll bet you would find that you sleep better when you finally do go back to bed."

"Sometimes when I'm uptight, I like to get a good work-out," said Al.

"That's an excellent idea. You can displace some of that worry with physical activity. When I do that, I'm much more relaxed afterward.

"One more way you can displace worry is to take the negative thoughts and shove them aside with positive thoughts. For example, I might worry about the exam having surprise questions that I'm not prepared to answer. But I can shove those thoughts aside by reminding myself that I've taken many exams and I've handled surprise questions before. I have learned the material, so all I have to do is show the prof what I know."

"I've tried that," said Joanne, "but sometimes those negative thoughts keep coming back. What do you do then?"

"That's where I go to the third option: *Treat the symptoms*. Sometimes you can't eliminate the worry so you have to try to alleviate the worst elements of it. One way to do that is to keep things in perspective. Jo, is there one final you're worried about more than the others?"

"Economics. Everyone says Bolger's tests are the hardest on campus."

"Let's use that for an example. What's the worst you could do on the test?"

She thought for a moment. "Well, based on the fact that I've attended every class, I've taken good notes, and I've studied the textbook thoroughly, I can't imagine getting worse than a *C*. Actually, I think I could go in and get a *B*."

"You can ace it," said Al.

"But the worst is probably a *C*," said Dave. "And it wouldn't take much to get a *B*. Now how bad is that?"

"Actually, after I heard everyone talk about Dr. Bolger at the first of the year, I didn't expect to do better than a *B* when I started the course. I have a solid *B* right now, and if I do well on the test, I have a chance for an *A*."

"And that's from someone who 'doesn't give *A*'s!' You've done an outstanding job. Keep that in mind. A healthy perspective on a situation treats the symptoms of worry.

"Now suppose you were actually looking at a *D*, or worse, when you honestly evaluated your chances on the exam. And that really made you uptight. You can't eliminate the cause or displace the thoughts. What would you do?"

"I could drop the course," laughed Joanne.

"That's an option. What's another possibility?"

"I could get some help."

"And where would you find that help?"

"Well, I could find someone in the class who understands what is going on and study with him or her. Or I might even go and talk to the professor."

"Good. So talking to people and getting help treats the symptoms of worry. Actually, as you are receiving help, you might find yourself back at the second technique, displacing the thoughts. With time and improvement, you might even eliminate the cause of the worry."

"Dave, I really appreciate this," said Al. "You're showing me how to handle my excessive anxiety. But I'm wondering if maybe a little bit of worry isn't a good idea. When I go out to play a basketball game, I'm always a little nervous. In fact, I don't play well without some butterflies in the stomach. Not too many, but I do need some."

"That's an excellent point. Those butterflies before a game serve an important function. They help you focus totally on the job at hand, and pump some extra adrenaline through your body to help you get maximum performance. That's exactly how we want to be for finals, prepared to give our very best effort.

"The question is how do we reach that ultimate in preparation and alertness? Here's one suggestion:

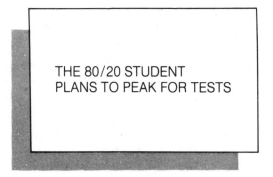

THE 80/20 STUDENT
PLANS TO PEAK FOR TESTS

"When I say we want to peak for exams, I'm talking about focusing and supercharging our minds. Now that we've dealt with the problem of worry, we're free to fill our minds with the things that will help us at the time of the exam.

"First, let's talk a little about memory. We have various levels of memory. There's what's called short-term memory. If I gave you a phone number, you'd remember it for about 45 seconds. You also have an intermediate memory. Joanne, if I asked what you did yesterday afternoon, you could pretty well account for every hour of your time. But how about three months ago? You might remember what you did in general, but you probably couldn't give an hour-by-hour account for each day. Long-term memory is keyed to vividly memorable events, such as the day my father died. I can recall every moment of that morning.

"Understanding how our memory functions helps us prepare for exams. My preparation is geared to maximizing my use of each aspect of my memory capability. Let me emphasize — my goal is to supercharge the mind rather than fry my emotions. So I don't stay up all night because I need to be alert for the exam."

"You probably reach a point where your productivity declines, anyway," said Al.

"That's right. As we've said before, it's important to utilize our strengths. What I do is saturate my mind with as much information as possible the night before an exam. Then I go to bed, get a good night's sleep and refresh my mind in the morning."

"Do you think it's good to study with someone for exams?" asked Joanne.

"Sometimes. It would be helpful to quiz each other on potential questions you may face on an exam. But I also need time alone to pack that information into my mind."

"Is that when you use those summary boxes in your notes?"

"Yes, that is part of my review process. The night before the test, I'm supercharging my intermediate memory. I pay particular attention to the main points in my 80/20 notes, reviewing what the instructor emphasized. I review the text in the same way. The summary notes are a good thing to review again in the morning, for they're the pithy essence of each class.

"In fact, I'm reviewing right up to the last minute. I usually bring my notes to the test and try to make maximum use of my short-term memory. At the last minute I review any crucial facts and information. My goal is to recall and write that information immediately when the test starts. I go through the questions as quickly as possible and note any initial thoughts beside each question. You can often pick up quite a few points that way. Sometimes I end up with almost an outline of my answer just from these first thoughts. When I come back later to write it, I might be able to harvest my mind for even more ideas because I have 'loaded' it at the first of the exam.

"By the way, there is no rule that says you have to answer the first question first. If you sense a burst of creativity coming on some other question, follow through — write that answer right away."

"I never thought of doing that," said Joanne. "I've always started at the beginning. If I didn't get something, I'd go on and come back to it if I had time."

"That's another good point," Dave stated. "Don't get stuck on one question. Remember that your objective is to show the professor what you know. If your thoughts aren't clicking on one question, you are probably wasting your time. Move on to a question where you can be more productive.

"In fact, that's a very important point. We've stated it before, but it bears repeating:

ON EXAMS: *ALWAYS* SHOW WHAT YOU KNOW

"We can use the BAM outline here," said Al.

"You're exactly right. The same principles that apply when we talk in class and do our homework apply here. We want to *Be,* that is be neat and have well-organized answers. And we've talked some already about *Anticipate*. That's planning, so we're not just presenting information at random. It's not a bad idea on some tests to keep a scratch paper handy so you can jot down an outline or make a checklist of the points you want to cover in an answer, or perhaps try a couple of approaches on a proof if you're not quite sure of the solution.

"And finally there's *Motivate*. Be as interesting and creative as you can in your limited time. Just as in your papers, you try to have an interesting opening and close, and to convey enthusiasm for your subject, do the same when you have to answer an essay question.

"Go for partial credit when you don't know the answer in full. On true/false and multiple choice questions, always make a guess if there is no penalty for wrong answers.

"Show what you *do* know. I'll never forget one exam I took in advanced calculus at State Tech that really illustrates the value of going for partial credit."

"I sympathize already," said Al. "I like math, but that's one tough course."

"On my final," Dave continued, "there was one proof on which I started at the top and got through several steps before I got stuck. I didn't know where to go from there, so I went down to the conclusion and started writing, working my way back up toward my first steps. But I couldn't link the two halves; there seemed to be a gap. Yet I hoped to get at least some partial credit from both parts of what I wrote. When I got the paper back, the professor apparently saw the connection and gave me full credit! I still have no idea what the connection was.

"That experience also illustrates a very important principle. What if you're not sure of an answer? I want the professor to know what I'm thinking. If I just put down the conclusion and I'm wrong, then I receive no credit. So I write down every thought that might be pertinent. I write as much as I can as fast as I can. I don't mind filling several blue books if I have to. If I don't know an answer, I lay a framework for an answer. Even if my conclusion is wrong, the professor can see my reasoning, and maybe some of that is right. I'm a master at getting partial credit."

"Dave, this is really good advice," Joanne volunteered. "One of my biggest problems is that I have to memorize so many facts for my economics final. Could we talk more about that long-term memory you mentioned?"

"Okay, let's talk about that. How can we put something in our brain so it will stay for some time, certainly beyond twenty-four hours? Here's a principle I use to help me do that:

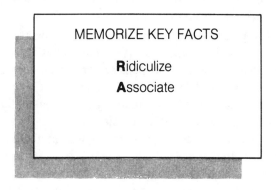

MEMORIZE KEY FACTS

Ridiculize

Associate

"Ridiculize isn't a word," protested Joanne.

"It's not in the dictionary, but it says exactly what you need to do. Let me see if we can illustrate what I mean. Does either of you remember the three points on how to be creative that we talked about a few weeks ago?"

"Yes, I remember all three clearly," Al commented. "In fact, I really appreciated the farming illustration you gave."

"Exactly, Al. You remember because I used an unusual illustration. That's what 'ridiculize' is all about. Joanne, can you give me some examples of facts you need to memorize for economics?"

Joanne pulled out her notebook. "Here are some. There are five important pieces of anti-trust legislation. I need to remember the names, in what order they were enacted, and what they were designed to accomplish. I think I can remember the dates if I can just keep them in the right order."

"May I see those five pieces of legislation?"

Joanne showed Dave the list:

Sherman Act, 1890
Clayton Act, 1914
Robinson-Patman Act, 1936
Miller-Tydings Act, 1937
Celler Antimerger Act, 1950

"Now you're sure you don't need to memorize the exact dates?"

"No, what's most important is that we know the name of the acts, their sequence, and what each one accomplished."

"Good, because dates are a little more complicated. There are some good books on memory that can teach you techniques for memorizing dates and numbers."

Dave leaned back, closed his eyes and released his imagination. "This will be fun. Let's start with the Sherman Antitrust Act. Imagine a big Sherman tank. It's firing the first round of the antitrust war. Flying out of the tank's gun in a long arc is a gigantic, one-ton lump of clay. That's for the Clayton Act. If I remember, its purpose was to strengthen the Sherman Act. So, on that lump of clay, imagine some bulging muscles. Now, where is this lump of clay going to land?"

"Right next to Jackie Robinson!" said Al.

"Ever heard of him, Joanne?"

"Of course. The first black baseball player in the major leagues."

"Picture Jackie Robinson scared by the huge lump of clay landing near him. He's running hard to escape, and as he does, he's reaching out his hand and patting a man on the back. Robinson-Patman. What was the purpose of that bill?"

Jo glanced at her notes. "To control chain stores."

"Picture the man Robinson is patting holding a huge link chain, and inside each link is a grocery store. Got the picture?"

"Yes!" Joanne couldn't help giggling. "It's funny."

"That's the idea. The crazier the better. Next is Miller-Tydings. What's a miller? Someone who operates a mill. He makes flour. Picture that chain winding its way over into this mill and the miller is all covered with flour and he's cheerfully and enthusiastically waving glad tidings. Miller-Tydings."

"That bill was to control retail prices. How about the miller's other hand on a big cash register and dollar signs are flying out of it," Joanne suggested.

"Great!" Dave exclaimed, "You're getting the idea."

Joanne was on a roll now. "And those dollar signs are moving, kind of like smoke, through a door and down into a cellar." Then she stopped. "Now how do I remember what the Celler Act does?" Jo looked at her notes again. "It closed a loophole in the law and prohibited mergers by competing companies when the effect was to lessen competition."

"Hm. Okay, how about another cellar with a huge mouth, about to gobble up the first cellar. And the first cellar has a big hand up and it's shouting 'No!'"

"That's incredible! I've got it."

"You got it. *I* got it!" said Al. "I'm not taking the test and there's no way I'm going to forget it."

Everyone laughed. It seemed that all the tension was gone. Sure exams were approaching, but there was a quiet confidence exuding from the students as they realized they knew exactly what they had to do to prepare.

"Well, Mentor, I guess our assignment is pretty obvious."

"I could say good luck. But you don't need that. I'm expecting great things. By the way, my wife and I would like to have you two over for dinner after finals. She's curious to hear more about what we're doing. And it would give us a chance to review everything, and celebrate your success.

Both students eagerly agreed. Home-cooked meals were a special treat for students living on campus. They set the date for the night before the start of the new term.

12

THE COMPLETE 80/20 STUDENT: PUTTING IT ALL TOGETHER

"This is the best meal I've had in months!" said Al as he accepted a third helping of chicken and mashed potatoes. "They sure don't cook like this in my dorm." Al and Joanne had received their grades earlier in the day, making dinner with Dave and his wife, Mary, a festive occasion. Al had aced his history test, improving his overall grade to a solid *B* for the term. His *B* average was a one-point increase over that of his freshman year. Joanne had achieved an *A-* average, including an *A* in Dr. Bolger's economics class. Her overall increase was seven-tenths of a point. Both remembered how Dave had promised a one-half to one-point increase in their grade point averages if they faithfully practiced what he taught them.

Mary wanted to know what caused the improvement. "What did you talk about at those meetings every week?"

Since Al was still eating, Joanne spoke first. "I think I've really learned how to study. In high school, I got straight *A*s because I worked a little harder than most of my classmates. And I think I was probably above average in intelligence; they considered me a brain. But at the university, I found myself competing with people just as smart and dedicated as I was. That's when I realized that my study habits weren't as good as I thought. Dave has taught me how to learn."

"We've become 80/20 Students!" said Al as he wiped his mouth, then leaned back and patted his stomach. "I'm glad I don't have practice tonight. I don't think I'll be able to move for awhile. When Dave first told us about the 80/20

Rule, I was skeptical. It had a ring of truth, but I wondered if it was really practical. During the term, Dave helped me become better organized. Because I'm studying more in the morning when I'm most alert, and thinking more aggressively in class, I have more time to do other things I enjoy. And my grades are better. You can't beat that combination!"

"That rule has really been a help to me, too," said Joanne. "I used to spend endless hours trying to read my assigned books. Now I spend a fraction of the time and get a lot more out of them. I never would have guessed that just a few new techniques could be so effective."

"Me too!" Al interrupted. "I am amazed at how much less time it takes me to get to the root of problems and to make decisions. Both my friends and my professors are amazed, too. What's more, I'm even learning to be creative. I can't begin to measure how much more effective I am in homework and in class due to better ideas."

"I really work smarter now, not just harder like I used to," Joanne added. "I used to be overwhelmed by so many school activities — but I had no plan. Now I have a focus. I'm involved in only a portion of the activities I used to be in, but I plan so that every one of them contributes toward my success in school. For the first time, I feel relaxed and on top of things."

"This really must be some concept. What exactly does an 80/20 Student do?" asked Mary.

"Glad you asked!" said Al. With a flourish he rose from the table. "Joanne, it's time to present the chart."

Joanne produced a roll of paper which Al helped her unfurl for Dave and Mary. "I had 23 three-by-five cards on my wall at the end of the term," explained Al. "Each of them is simple and understandable. They don't usually take any more time than we already spend studying or attending class. So Jo and I thought it might be a good idea to combine all of those cards into one chart we could put over our desks. Kind of a giant crib sheet to help us remember and apply what you taught us. We haven't actually completed it, but we thought you'd like to see what we've developed so far."

Mary suggested that they move into the living room so the two students could spread the chart on the coffee table. Across the top of the paper were the words, "How to be an 80/20 Student" and and underneath was the 80/20 Rule: "80 percent of the benefit from school can be gained by doing the right 20 percent of the activity well."

"That's the overall concept of the 80/20 Student," Al explained. "Jo and I took our cards and spread them out, much like we do when we write papers. You'll notice we have divided the chart into three columns."

Joanne took over the commentary, "On the left side of the chart we placed the three main techniques we have used the most often — in class, on homework and on tests. We decided to use "Think With 80/20 Aggressiveness" as the first one, the general title for SAFE, the outline which was used in different ways."

THINK WITH 80/20 AGGRESSIVENESS

When thinking, listening, reading and observing:

Scan

Ask

Focus

Explore

SEEK 80/20 FACTS

When thinking with 80/20 aggressiveness, seek:

Causes

Objectives

Priorities

PRESENT WITH 80/20 IMPACT

Show what you know:

Be

Anticipate

Motivate

"In the middle column," Al continued, "we placed six more techniques which we have used frequently in one or more types of situation. These aren't quite as basic as the three main techniques, but they are very important."

SIX MORE 80/20 TECHNIQUES

1. Ask Good Questions

    Clarifying
    Applying
    Tying

2. Be Creative

    Cultivate creative thinking
    Harvest the mind
       Load
       Relax
       Capture
    Push mental boundaries

3. Deal with Worries

    Delete the causes
    Displace the thoughts
    Treat the symptoms

4. Memorize Key Facts

    Ridiculize
    Associate

5. Learn to Like What You Do

Remember why
Enlist a friend
Make a game of it

6. Chart Decisions

Alternatives

		A	B	C
	1	+	−	+
Objectives	2	0	0	−
	3	+	+	0

Joanne picked up: "In the right column we arranged all the remaining principles and techniques you gave us according to the setting where they are used: in class, on homework and on tests. A few of them were more general so we added that category. Since this column provides a how-to checklist of what we are to do in the most common student settings, we decided to repeat the three main techniques and the six others where appropriate in these lists, just as helpful reminders."

WHERE AND HOW TO USE 80/20 TECHNIQUES

In Class:

*Always attend
*Determine class objectives
*Think with 80/20 aggressiveness
*Seek 80/20 facts

*Keep structured notes

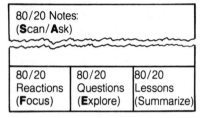

80/20 Notes: (**S**can/**A**sk)		
80/20 Reactions (**F**ocus)	80/20 Questions (**E**xplore)	80/20 Lessons (Summarize)

*Ask good questions
*Present with 80/20 impact

On Homework

*Turn it it
*Think with 80/20 aggressiveness
*Seek 80/20 facts
*Present with 80/20 impact
*Follow standard paper schedule
*Be creative

On Tests

*Plan to peak
*Deal with worries
*Memorize key facts
*Think with 80/20 aggressiveness
*Seek 80/20 facts
*Present with 80/20 impact

In General

*Make the most of your strengths
*Find help for your weaknesses
*Learn to like what you do
*Chart decisions

"As you can see, we've refined some of the wording to make the concepts as simple and easy to remember as possible," said Al. "Also, Joanne suggested that we put 'Trust God for Peace and Wisdom' along the bottom as the foundation principle."

"I think that was the highlight for me," she said, stopping to control her emotions. "When you shared how God helped you when your dad died. . . I've thought a lot about that, and I'd have to say that is the most important thing I've learned. You didn't have us put it on a three-by-five card, but it seemed to me that it was the foundation of all the other things you said."

"That point has been growing on me too, Dave," Al admitted. "Thanks for being so open with us."

"You're quite welcome, Al." Dave was pleased with Al's and Joanne's words and he was moved by their sincerity. "That's a tremendous insight. The Bible has a great deal to say about gaining peace and wisdom. If God created our minds, then it is to our benefit to understand how He wants us to use them.

"And let me commend you for the tremendous job you two have done on this chart. You've really captured the essence of what I've been teaching you."

"We've tried to make this easy to remember," said Al. "You gave us a couple of acrostics such as SAFE and BAM. They help us remember how to think with 80/20 aggressiveness and present with 80/20 impact."

"We felt there was another area you covered, and that's the area of facts," Joanne continued. "When we're scanning, asking, focusing and exploring, just what are we looking for? And what are we presenting when we 'Be, Anticipate and Motivate'? We came up with 'Seek 80/20 Facts.' The acrostic is COP — Causes, Objectives and Priorities. But we're not completely satisfied with that."

"Did we leave off anything important?" asked Al.

Dave studied the diagram. "It's very thorough," he said. "I wonder if we can improve that acrostic for seeking facts?" He thought for a couple of minutes. "How about COPE? We can cope in school if we know what facts to seek. I see four crucial types of facts to look for, particularly in the focus stage. The first two are the same — Causes and Objectives. Let the P stand for 'Patterns,' and let's have the E stand for 'Eighty-twenties.' Isn't that another way to say priorities?"

"Sure!" said Joanne. "The whole idea of the 80/20 Rule is prioritizing the activities, or seeking to do the right 20 percent of the activity well."

"But what do you mean by patterns?" asked Al.

"We never did put it on an index card," said Dave. "But this chart demonstrates that you understand the concept. It's the principle of making linkages between ideas."

"What does that mean?" asked Joanne.

"Remember the first time we met, when all the students were talking about their frustrations in school? I noted that you seemed to be saying that you had to either work hard at getting good grades and sacrifice having fun, or have fun and sacrifice the grades. That was a pattern I observed. I tried to organize what was being said, make some connections, and draw some conclusions.

"We used that principle in the note-taking outline, in the bottom three boxes. We looked for how the notes we took related to the course objectives and to other information we'd learned. I believe this is the essence of the learning process. There are many more ways to relate things than people imagine. Maybe you saw that when we discussed creativity, Al. When we were trying to help you be more creative with your papers, we were practicing this concept."

"I think I learned how to do that in my reading this year," said Joanne. "Rather than just learning the facts about a book, I was thinking more about the big picture, how incidents in a book related to historical events, and the influence of a writer's culture and philosophy on his work."

"That's it exactly. There are so many ways to look for patterns. Connections is another word we could use. In business I'm always trying to make connections according to our company objectives. I'm looking at every aspect of the business in terms of purpose, goals, usefulness, and so on. You can look for patterns among people, according to their physical characteristics or skills. We can look for

connections according to time, sequence, location, or parts
of a whole — which is what you did with this chart. You
saw the overall concept of the 80/20 Student and attempted
to fit all the parts — the three-by-five cards — into the one
whole."

"I'm truly impressed," said Mary, as she took one more
look at the chart. "I can see why you're so excited. Now
if you'll excuse me, I'd like to clear the table so we can
have dessert."

Dave suggested they go to his study. "I'd like to show
you what I call my 'time management system.' " The three
made their way down the hall to Dave's den. On two sides
of the room were bookshelves and a third wall was dominated
by a large stand-up desk.

"You really do work standing up," said Joanne.

"I sure do. I have another desk like this, only larger, in
my office at work."

Al noticed a thin 8½" x 11" calendar notebook on the
desk. "Is this how you schedule your time?"

"Well, that is part of it. I keep track of commitments on
those monthly calendars. You'll note that each page covers
an entire month. I don't count on my memory to record
important due dates." Dave got out the page for the previous
term and pointed out where he'd marked due dates for papers
and exams, as well as important family functions. "As you
can see, I don't just put the due date for a paper. For me,
the crucial date for a paper is the starting date. You'll note
how I've marked 'concept' for a major paper two weeks
before the final draft due date. If I keep track of starting
and ending points on a paper, I generally stay out of trouble."

Month **DECEMBER** 19___

SUNDAY	MONDAY	TUESDAY	WEDNESDAY	THURSDAY	FRIDAY	SATURDAY
	0	8 Car— Tune Up `1`	FIN Test `2` MKT Simulation exercise (report concept)	STAT Prob. `3` Set O.B. paper final draft	WAC `4` final draft	`5`
`6`	WAC `7` Concept PROD Project concept FIN reading Assign.	O.B. `8` Disc. group 4-6 Dentist	MKT `9` Simulation report final draft	STAT `10` Prob. Set	WAC `11` finaldraft Sam visits (eve.)	Men's `12` breakfast (church)
`13`	WAC `14` Concept	O.B. `15` group project report	FIN test `16`	STAT prob `17` Set 6-8 John's Birthday party	WAC final `18` draft PROD project final draft Thesis outline MKT test	Drive to `19` Mom's + Dad's for Christmas vacation

"That's amazing," said Al. "I never thought of doing that. I just keep all those things in my individual notebooks for each class."

"That's fine if you look at the notebooks each day."

"Well, I really don't."

"I suggest you get something like this so you can log your commitments and keep track of them all in one place. Then be sure to check the calendar every day."

Joanne asked, "Where is your class schedule?"

Dave flipped the calendar notebook open to the inside of the front cover. "Here is my standard week — including classes, family time, study time, etc."

Standard Weekly Schedule—Fall Semester

	SUN	MON	TUE	WED	THU	FRI	SAT
5	Exer., Shower and Devo.						
6	Special Bible	Study (Home)					Breakfast (out)
7	Study Breakfast	Breakfast (Home)					Thesis Research
8	Family	Travel (to camp.)					
9	— — — — — —	FIN 535	Study (Lib.)	FIN 535	Study (Lib.)	FIN 535	
10	Church	MKT 607	O.B. 602	MKT 607	O.B. 602	MKT 607	
11		Study (Lib.)	STAT 501	Study (Lib.)	STAT 501	Study (Lib.)	
12	Lunch	Lunch (cam.)					Lunch
1	Rest	PROD 520	Study (Lib.)	PROD 520	Study (Lib.)	PROD 520	Family
2		Study (lib.)		Study (Lib.)	Al + Joanne	WAC	
3	Home Projects					Discussion	
4					Study (home)		
5	Supper (home)						
6	Church	Supper (cam.)	Supper (home)				
7		Written Case Informal Discussion Group	Family				
8							
9							
10							

Joanne noticed, "I see you blocked out your standard appointments with Al and me. You're pretty organized."

"I use the 80/20 Rule here, too. There are a lot of things I can do in a day. But probably 20 percent of my activity will yield 80 percent of the results. So I arrange major blocks of time for my highest priority activities."

Al noted that Dave wrote "family" on his schedule. Dave explained that on most days the time from about 6 until his children go to bed around 9 is devoted to supper and other activities with the family. "My family is very important, but if I don't set aside time for them, the pressure of work and school could easily take me away from them. So I schedule it. Another thing I do is to leave an hour unscheduled each afternoon. That allows me flexibility if some project takes longer than anticipated or something comes up that I hadn't expected."

"Like the car breaking down," noted Joanne.

"That's right. Or perhaps one of my kids has an ear infection and I have to take him to the doctor. Or Mary needs me to run an errand at the store. I need that flexibility."

"I see you've got a file cabinet here," said Al. "That's not all for school work, is it?"

"No, actually only one drawer is for school." Dave pulled it open to show how he had files for each course he was taking.

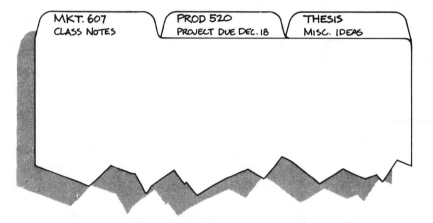

MKT. 607
CLASS NOTES

PROD 520
PROJECT DUE DEC. 18

THESIS
MISC. IDEAS

"I need to develop a better system," said Joanne.

"What system are you using right now?"

Joanne laughed. "Piles. I have my books on one side of the desk. Then I have these piles for each class. Actually, some of the piles get stacked on top of each other to give me room to work."

"How do you keep them straight?" Dave queried.

"I stagger them."

"I've tried that approach," said Al. "Unfortunately a few weeks into the term, they all get pushed into one stack."

"And then you're in trouble," said Dave. "You have no visible means of follow-up unless you go through the stack every day. I understand what you're doing. My system kind of evolved from that. When I first started college, I had no system. I tried the piles. Then I went to a folder system — one for each class. Now I have several files for each course. Notice I keep these in the file cabinet, and not out on my desk. I rely on my schedule, not my stacks, to tell me what to do next."

Dave pulled out a file titled "Thesis — ideas." "I found I needed to design what I call 'capture systems.' Remember how we discussed harvesting the mind — load, relax, capture? I used to write my ideas on slips of paper, but then I'd misplace those pieces of paper. Now an idea gets written on a card and slipped into a file. This file is for my thesis. I've been putting ideas in here all along. I have another file into which I'm putting pieces of research for that thesis. I have files for various projects in each class.

"Sometimes I vary the system to fit the class." Dave pulled out a notebook from the file drawer. "In one class I took last term, the instructor gave us a new case study at the end of each class period. They were already three-hole punched so I put them in this notebook. My class notes are also included with each case. All I had to do for the test was review this notebook."

Al was looking over the desk and noticed a "To do" list with today's date on it. "I have one of these," he said, "but it doesn't seem to do me much good."

"Why not?"

"I don't know. I get some things checked off, but as I get behind. . .I guess I don't feel I'm getting the most important things done."

"Do you notice the numbers I've put by each of the items?

Priority	Due Date	Status	**Study Time** Priority Activities Date: DEC. 14
4	14	✓	WAC Concept
3	15	✓	O.B. Group Project Rpt. Prep.
5	16	✓	FIN Test Preparation
7	17		STAT Problem Set.
9	18		PROD Project (finish draft first)
8	18		Thesis Outline Finalization
10	18		MKT Test Preparation
6	15	✓	STAT Req. Reading Assign.
1	14	✓	MKT Req. Case Study
2	14	✓	PROD Req Case Study
			OTHER TIME PRIORITY ACTIVITIES
1	17	✓	Buy John's Birthday Present
2	18	✓	Get ready for trip home

"I don't just make a list. I apply the 80/20 Rule to the list. For example, I determine my priority activities for the study time blocks I have available during the day. Reading and analyzing my marketing case study was the number one priority for December 14. I started with that and kept at it until I was done. Next I went on to the number two priority and kept at that until it was done. You can see that when I finished that day, I hadn't checked off items 7 through 10. But I knew I'd done the things that were of highest priority, and those last four items got carried over to the next day."

Suddenly Dave stepped back toward the door. "I just thought of something!" he said, and pointed to the calendar notebook on the desk. "Note commitments right away." Then he pointed to the standard weekly schedule. "Arrange your standard week." He next pointed to the file cabinet. "Put your stacks in files." And finally he referred to his "to do" list. "Start top priority first. What does the first letter of those four points spell? NAPS! Do all this and you'll have enough time even for naps occasionally."

MANAGE YOUR TIME

Note commitments right away

Arrange your standard week

Put your stacks in files

Start top priority first

Joanne burst out laughing. "Dave, you're too much!"

"Hey, let's add that as a seventh 80/20 technique in the middle column of our chart, Joanne," Al suggested.

"Good idea, Al."

Dave asked, "Then how about your doing a final version of the chart and giving copies to Joanne and me?" (See pages 136-137 for a copy of the final chart, which may be photocopied for your personal use.)

Mary called the group back to the dining room for dessert. As they sat down to enjoy a fresh-baked apple pie, a la mode, Joanne said, "You know one thing I'm going to miss? There was something about meeting every week that was extremely helpful. Just knowing that we were going to get together in a few days and check up on how we were doing seemed to make me work better."

"That's a very sound observation," said Dave. "It's the principle of accountability. I won't make you write it on a three-by-five card, but you should remember it. Maybe you should add it to the chart.

BE ACCOUNTABLE TO SOMEONE

"This principle worked for me this past term, too. As your mentor, I was highly motivated to practice what I was teaching you. It made me a better student. And as we discussed various principles and techniques, I improved some of my skills in the process."

"I don't suppose it would be right to keep meeting this term," Joanne said hesitantly.

"No, I think I've done about all I can to help you. However, there's no reason you can't turn around and meet with another student or two and hold each other accountable. Or better yet, teach what you've learned to someone else."

"I think I hear one last three-by-five card for this course!" said Al.

"What's that?" asked Joanne.

THE 80/20 STUDENT HELPS
OTHERS BECOME 80/20
STUDENTS

"I think we'll add that to the chart, too," Al said.

"I like that," said Dave with a smile. "There's something special about helping others become successful. I would love to see everyone on this campus be an 80/20 Student."

"I know I've become one, and I don't want to stop," said Joanne.

"Becoming an 80/20 Student has been fantastic, unbelievable, and natural!" She looked at Al with a sly grin. "Did you catch what that spells?"

Al was a bit puzzled. "Fantastic. . .Unbelievable. . .Natural. I've got it. FUN!"

Everyone laughed. "You're absolutely right," said Dave. "That's what we've been learning all these weeks: How to get better grades. . ."

Joanne and Al joined him and they finished the phrase together:

". . .and have more FUN!"

HOW TO GET BETTER GRADES AND HAVE MORE FUN
How to be an 80/20 Student

THE 80/20 RULE: 80 percent of the benefit from school can be gained by doing the right 20 percent of the activity well.

THREE MAIN 80/20 TECHNIQUES	SEVEN MORE 80/20 TECHNIQUES	WHERE AND HOW TO USE 80/20 TECHNIQUES

THINK WITH 80/20 AGGRESSIVENESS
 	
When thinking, listening, reading and observing:
 	
Scan
 	
Ask
 	
Focus
 	
Explore
	ASK GOOD QUESTIONS
	
	Clarifying
	Applying
	Tying
	
	BE CREATIVE
	
	Cultivate creative thinking
	Harvest the mind
	   Load
	   Relax
	   Capture
	Push mental boundaries
		IN CLASS
		
		• Always attend
		• Determine class objectives
		• Think With 80/20 Aggressiveness
		• Seek 80/20 Facts
		• Keep structured notes:

SEEK 80/20 FACTS When thinking with 80/20 aggressiveness, seek:	**DEAL WITH WORRIES** **D**elete the causes **D**isplace the thoughts **T**reat the symptoms	

80/20 Notes: (**S**can/**A**sk)

80/20 Reactions (**F**ocus/ COPE)	80/20 Questions (**E**xplore/ CAT)	80/20 Lessons (Summarize)

• Ask Good Questions
• Present With 80/20 Impact

ON HOMEWORK

- Turn it in
- Concept/Research/Outline/First Draft/ Major Edit/Final Draft
- Think With 80/20 Aggressiveness
- Seek 80/20 Facts
- Present With 80/20 Impact
- Be Creative

ON TESTS

- Plan to peak
- Deal With Worries
- Memorize Key Facts
- Think With 80/20 Aggressiveness
- Seek 80/20 Facts
- Present With 80/20 Impact

IN GENERAL

- Make the most of your strengths
- Find help for your weaknesses
- Learn to Like What You Do
- Chart Decisions
- Manage Your Time
- Be accountable to someone
- Help others become 80/20 Students

MEMORIZE KEY FACTS

Ridiculize
Associate

LEARN TO LIKE WHAT YOU DO

Remember why
Enlist a friend
Make a game of it

CHART DECISIONS

		Alternatives		
		A	B	C
Objectives	1	+	−	+
	2	0	0	−
	3	+	+	0

MANAGE YOUR TIME

Note commitments right away
(homework, tests, appointments, other)
Arrange your standard week
Put your stacks in files
Start top priority first

Causes
(symptoms → causes)

Objectives
(what vs. how)

Patterns
(linkages)

Eighty/Twenties
(priorities)

PRESENT WITH 80/20 IMPACT

Show what you know.

Be

Anticipate

Motivate

TRUST GOD FOR PEACE AND WISDOM

APPENDIX

This is the booklet mentioned on page 106 that Dave gave to Joanne and Al.

HAVE YOU HEARD
OF THE
FOUR SPIRITUAL LAWS?

Just as there are physical laws that govern the physical universe, so are there spiritual laws which govern your relationship with God.

LAW ONE

GOD **LOVES** YOU, AND OFFERS A WONDERFUL **PLAN** FOR YOUR LIFE.

GOD'S LOVE

"For God so loved the world, that He gave His only begotten Son, that whoever believes in Him should not perish, but have eternal life." (John 3:16).

GOD'S PLAN

(Christ speaking) "I came that they might have life, and might have it abundantly" (that it might be full and meaningful) (John 10:10).

> Why is it that most people are
> not experiencing the abundant life?
> Because. . .

LAW TWO

MAN IS **SINFUL** AND **SEPARATED** FROM GOD, THUS, HE CANNOT KNOW AND EXPERIENCE GOD'S LOVE AND PLAN FOR HIS LIFE.

MAN IS SINFUL

"For all have sinned and fall short of the glory of God" (Romans 3:23).

Man was created to have fellowship with God; but, because of his own stubborn self-will, he chose to go his own independent way and fellowship with God was broken. This self-will, characterized by an attitude of active rebellion or passive indifference, is an evidence of what the Bible calls sin.

MAN IS SEPARATED

"For the wages of sin is death" (spiritual separation from God) (Romans 6:23).

This diagram illustrates that God is holy and man is sinful. A great gulf separates the two. The arrows illustrate that man is continually trying to reach God and the abundant life through his own effort, such as a good life, philosophy or religion.

The Third Law explains the only
way to bridge this gulf. . .

LAW THREE

JESUS CHRIST IS GOD'S ONLY PROVISION FOR MAN'S SIN. THROUGH HIM YOU CAN KNOW AND EXPERIENCE GOD'S LOVE AND PLAN FOR YOUR LIFE.

HE DIED IN OUR PLACE

"But God demonstrates His own love toward us, in that while we were yet sinners, Christ died for us" (Romans 5:8).

HE ROSE FROM THE DEAD

"Christ died for our sins. . .he was buried. . .He was raised on the third day according to the Scriptures. . .He appeared to Peter, then to the twelve. After that He appeared to more than five hundred. . ." (I Corinthians 15:3-6).

HE IS THE ONLY WAY TO GOD

"Jesus said to him, 'I am the way, and the truth and the life; no one comes to the Father, but through Me'" (John 14:6).

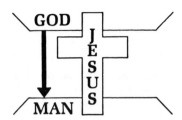

This diagram illustrates that God has bridged the gulf which separates us from Him by sending His Son, Jesus Christ, to die on the cross in our place to pay the penalty for our sins.

> It is not enough to know these three laws
> nor even to give intellectual assent to them. . .

LAW FOUR

WE MUST INDIVIDUALLY **RECEIVE** JESUS CHRIST AS SAVIOR AND LORD; THEN WE CAN KNOW AND EXPERIENCE GOD'S LOVE AND PLAN FOR OUR LIVES.

WE MUST RECEIVE CHRIST

"But as many as received Him, to them He gave the right to become children of God, even to those who believe in His name" (John 1:12).

WE RECEIVE CHRIST THROUGH FAITH

"For by grace you have been saved through faith; and that not of your selves, it is a gift of God; not as a result of works, that no one should boast" (Ephesians 2:8,9).

When We Receive Christ, We Experience a New Birth

(Read John 3:1-8.)

WE RECEIVE CHRIST BY PERSONAL INVITATION

(Christ is speaking) "Behold, I stand at the door and knock; if anyone hears My voice and opens the door, I will come in to him" (Revelation 3:20).

Receiving Christ involves turning to God from self (repentance) and trusting Christ to come into our lives to forgive our sins and to make us the kind of people He wants us to be. Just to agree intellectually that Jesus Christ is the Son of God and that He died on the cross for our sins is not enough. Nor is it enough to have an emotional experience. We receive Jesus Christ by faith, as an act of the will.

These two circles represent two kinds of lives:

SELF-DIRECTED LIFE

S — Self is on the throne

† — Christ is outside the life

● — Interests are directed by self, often resulting in discord and frustration

CHRIST-DIRECTED LIFE

† — Christ is in the life and on the throne

S — Self is yielding to Christ

● — Interests are directed by Christ, resulting in harmony with God's plan

Which circle best represents your life?

Which circle would you like to have represent your life?

The following explains how you can receive Christ:

YOU CAN RECEIVE CHRIST RIGHT NOW BY FAITH THROUGH PRAYER

(Prayer is talking with God)

God knows your heart and is not so concerned with your words as He is with the attitude of your heart. The following is a suggested prayer:

"Lord Jesus, I need You. Thank You for dying on the cross for my sins. I open the door of my life and receive You as my Savior and Lord. Thank You for forgiving my sins and giving me eternal life. Take control of the throne of my life. Make me the kind of person You want me to be."

Does this prayer express the desire of your heart?

If it does, pray this prayer right now, and Christ will come into your life, as He promised.

HOW TO KNOW THAT CHRIST IS IN YOUR LIFE

Did you receive Christ into your life? According to His promise in Revelation 3:20, where is Christ right now in relation to you? Christ said that He would come into your life. Would He mislead you? On what authority do you know that God has answered your prayer? (The trustworthiness of God Himself and His Word).

THE BIBLE PROMISES ETERNAL LIFE TO ALL WHO RECEIVE CHRIST

"And the witness is this, that God has given us eternal life, and this life is in His Son. He who has the Son has the life; he who does not have the Son of God does not have the life. These things I have written to you who believe in the name of the Son of God, in order that you may know that you have eternal life" (I John 5:11-13).

Thank God often that Christ is in your life and that He will never leave you (Hebrews 13:5). You can know on the basis of His promise that Christ lives in you and that you have eternal life, from the very moment you invite Him in. He will not deceive you.

MEET WITH OTHER CHRISTIANS

The Christian life was not meant to be lived alone. God's Word admonishes us not to forsake "the assembling of ourselves together . . ." (Hebrews 10:25). Several logs burn brightly together; but put one aside on the cold hearth and the fire goes out. So it is with your relationship to other Christians. If you do not belong to a church, do not wait to be invited. Take the initiative; call the pastor of a nearby church where Christ is honored and His Word is preached. Start this week, and make plans to attend regularly.

SPECIAL MATERIALS ARE AVAILABLE FOR CHRISTIAN GROWTH.

If you have established a relationship with God through Christ as you were reading the above, please write me and tell me about it. I would be delighted to send you some materials that will help you in your ongoing walk with God.

Steve Douglass
c/o Integrated Resources
100 Sunport Lane
Orlando, FL 32809